Web App Development

Web App Development

A Computer Science Approach

First Edition

Steve Beaty

Metropolitan State University of Denver

Bassim Hamadeh, CEO and Publisher
Christina Brown, Associate Acquisitions Editor
Kaela Martin, Senior Project Editor
Susana Christie, Senior Developmental Editor
Samantha Hansen, Production Editor
Jessica Delia, Graphic Design Associate
Kara Tatum, Licensing Coordinator
Natalie Piccotti, Director of Marketing
Kassie Graves, Senior Vice President, Editorial
Alia Bales, Director, Project Editorial and Production

Printed in the United States of America.

For Yang.

Contents

Preface ix

Chapter 1 An Overview of the Web 1

Chapter 2 Ruby for Rails 13

Chapter 3 Models 29

Chapter 4 Views 67

Chapter 5 Controllers 105

Chapter 6 Security 119

Appendix A Installation 133

Index 153

Preface

> "In an extreme view, the world can be seen as only connections, nothing else. We think of a dictionary as the repository of meaning, but it defines words only in terms of other words. I liked the idea that a piece of information is really defined only by what it's related to, and how it's related. There really is little else to meaning. The structure is everything. There are billions of neurons in our brains, but what are neurons? Just cells. The brain has no knowledge until connections are made between neurons. All that we know, all that we are, comes from the way our neurons are connected."
>
> Tim Berners-Lee

TL;DR

```
rails new Todo
cd Todo
rails generate scaffold item what:string when:date
rails db:migrate
rails server
# Surf to http://localhost:3000/items
```

Introduction

The web is ubiquitous. There is the obvious web, the one that uses browsers, URLs, and hyperlinks. But the web is larger than that. It encompasses all our devices, our phones, tablets, laptops, desktops, and Internet of Things devices.

It is behind many of the applications we use all the time, without our being directly aware of that fact. It powers social media sites and therefore connects us. It connects businesses to consumers and other businesses. It connects consumers to consumers via free or low-cost e-commerce sites. The protocols created for the web are the glue that holds many of our devices and computers together. Many of what appear to be desktop, native, applications are web applications running in browser environments that create the appearance of being fully integrated into our devices. One of the great powers of the web is that our browsers and web applications make the software easier to run in a wide variety of environments, somewhat easing the developer's burden while giving us familiar interfaces to that software.

This book will endeavor to cover the breadth of this very large field and give depth in areas where deep knowledge is necessary. It assumes you have a programming background and is targeted to upper-division college courses.

Audience

This book is intended to be used in colleges and universities for a computing degree at a sophomore level or above. Readers are expected to have at least two classes in a programming language before attempting this material. This book is appropriate for a one-quarter or semester class. This book is not about Ruby on Rails, this book is about how all web applications are developed; Ruby on Rails was simply chosen as an exemplar. Many computer science or software engineering concepts are covered and put into the context of web application development. As many, if not most, graduates with computing degrees will be employed creating web applications, having a web application development class in a college or university's curriculum has become more and more relevant. And as many, if not most, applications are web-based, it has become crucial to apply all our computer science and software engineering techniques to web application development.

Approach

Why Rails?

Well, why not? There is no be-all, end-all web framework, and Rails is better than many others for teaching the important aspects of web application frameworks. This is because, at least, of the following.

1. Rails is the progenitor for most other frameworks. It was created in 2003 and remains relevant today. Rails' approach and terminology has been adopted by many other frameworks.
2. Rails has evolved to respond to the changing nature of the web. The current version is 7 and it has many of the features that all modern web frameworks have.
3. Rails is portable across the usual platforms, in large part due to the fact Ruby is portable to those platforms.
4. Ruby and Rails have a large, crowd-sourced, support community. When we have a question, there are typically many enthusiastic people willing to address the question.
5. Similarly, it is very well supported. Both Rails and many of its associated gems are actively developed and supported.
6. It is widely used. A search of websites using Rails returns many of the most highly trafficked websites.
7. It is, for this book, simple. This book strives to discuss concepts without having details interfere with that discussion. Rails enhances understanding as it does what is needed, and nothing else. This is demonstrated in the following ways.
    a. Rails can create a running, usable application in very few steps.
    b. It doesn't require package managers beyond what Ruby requires, simplifying the usually

difficult task of managing package dependencies.

c. It integrates well with other tools such as git.

Computer Science

This book is designed to weave computer science concepts into the creation of web applications. You do not have to have a computer science degree to be a web application developer of course, but many graduates of computer science programs spend their careers developing web applications and the concepts presented here will help anyone who develops web, and other, applications.

Brevity is the Soul of Wit–Shakespeare

This book attempts to always use the minimum amount of commands and code required to demonstrate a concept. This means the fewest changes to applications that use the Rails' commands and using the fewest Ruby gems whenever possible. This will hopefully lead to the greatest compatibility and flexibility across platforms but might not always demonstrate all the capabilities of Rails or indeed of web applications. The hope is to show how to quickly create a running application with pointers to how it may be enhanced using other web technologies.

We'll use the default SQLite database for most of the book. It's small, lightweight, and very widely deployed. No, it isn't designed for high-volume web applications, but it works out of the box, and changing what database is used for a Rails application is a simple matter of configuration.

All frameworks are moving targets and this book uses the Rails 7 version to demonstrate web application development concepts; the details will change continuously and the companion website will be updated as appropriate.

Thanks

To Dr. Gearold Johnson, without whom I would not have had the great career and life I've had.

To Yaroslav Shmarov and his SupeRails Blog (https://blog.corsego.com/) for the autocomplete code that uses Hotwire's (https://hotwired.dev/) turbo-frame.

To everyone at Cognella, especially Kaela Martin, Christina Brown, Samantha Hansen, and Jessica Delia.

Conventions

Concept Leads to Code

You will find numerous Concept Leads to Code sections in what follows. These follow the overall approach of the book as we'll first discuss a general, Rails independent, concept and then show how the concept is implemented in Rails. It is the concepts that typically stick with us and are useful in a wide variety of programming contexts, seeing and doing working examples helps cement the concepts.

Typography

A monospaced font, `such as this`, will be used for all code examples, with commands and important comments **`in bold face.`**

Companion Website

There is a companion website at https://drb80.github.io/WebAppDev that contains references to Git repositories for much of the code in this book, database seed files, errata, etc. Comments are welcome at https://github.com/drb80/WebAppDev.

CHAPTER 1

An Overview of the Web

> *The original idea of the web was that it should be a collaborative space where you can communicate through sharing information.*
>
> Tim Berners-Lee

Introduction

The web is a technology that is so pervasive and easy to use that many don't have a firm grasp of its underpinnings. Those developing web applications must have a deep knowledge of the moving parts as the applications we create will use most of those parts. This chapter will start with a brief review of the creation and development of the web so we can appreciate its strengths and evolution. The chapter will also go into detail about the HyperText Transmission Protocol (HTTP) and its three versions as Rails, and other RESTful frameworks, make extensive use of the attributes of HTTP. These attributes include methods, headers, requests, and responses. As part of this examination, we'll look at the role Cookies and MIME types play in requests and responses. The chapter will introduce some browser tools crucial to the creation and debugging of web applications.

Learning Outcomes

By the end of this chapter, you'll be able to do the following.

1. Interact with and understand the request and response cycles web clients and servers use.
2. Debug your web applications using browser tools.
3. Interpret the protocol used to communicate the type of resource desired by a client and returned by a server.
4. Understand both accepted and error codes returned by servers for a requested resource.
5. Create resources that correspond to the RESTful paradigm, making your servers more scalable and cacheable.

Key Terms and Concepts

The following key terms and concepts will be introduced and/or used in this chapter.

1. **Protocol**
2. **Client/server**

3. **Request/response**
4. **Methods/verbs**
5. **Stateless communication**
6. **Representational State Transfer (REST)**
7. **Content Distribution Networks (CDNs)**

A Little History

In 1990 at Conseil Européen pour la Recherche Nucléaire (CERN), a high-energy physics laboratory, Tim Berners-Lee (TimBL) did something remarkable: he made the internet and its vast troves of information available to everyone for the first time. Before this, the internet was difficult to use for finding and sharing information. TimBL combined several technologies to make this remarkable change.

1. Standard Generalized Markup Language (SGML), the basis of the *Hyper Text Markup Language (HTML)*. HTML is used to describe how different parts of a web document are related to each other. More on this later.
2. *Hypertext*, is a term coined in 1963 by Ted Nelson to describe how documents can be connected to other documents via links. TimBL created Uniform Resource Locators (URLs) to create these links (see: Request For Comments (RFC) 1738).
3. **Client/server** network architecture. Here, a centralized server provides information to a wide number and types of software clients. Importantly, TimBL also created the *Hypertext Transfer Protocol (HTTP)* for communication between client and server. While relatively simple, HTTP captures what most clients (both people and other computers) need for effective communication. It also subsumes many other protocols because of its great flexibility. With the creation of one type of client, the browser, TimBL created a way for people with relatively little computer knowledge to access extraordinary amounts of data with ease.
4. *TCP/IP* networking and the *Internet*. Both predate the web by many years and allow for easy client/server connections.

The web wasn't the first attempt at information sharing. The *File Transfer Protocol (FTP)* was in wide use at the time, though finding resources wasn't part of the protocol itself. One had to know exactly what server, and directory on that server, where the desired data were. The *Wide Area Information Server (WAIS)* and *Gopher* were two other approaches to distributing and searching information that were popular around the time the web was created, but both fell from favor as the web expanded dramatically.

It's of course difficult to measure the size of the web: do we measure the number of servers, domains, and users? How accurately can we measure the number of users? Current estimates suggest that around 70% of the world's population use the web. From one user in 1990 to close to seven billion now—that's a doubling of users every year. Current estimates of the number of Internet of Things (IoT) devices (smart speakers, thermostats, light bulbs, doorbells, video cameras, etc.) have the total count of devices as being greater than the earth's population, with almost all of these being accessible through the web.

There has been an evolution of web browsers. The original web browser at CERN ("Nexus") also functioned as an editor—a functionality that presaged wikis. In the early 1990s, the National Center for

Supercomputer Applications (NCSA) at the University of Illinois Urbana-Champaign (UIUC) created both a browser (Mosaic) and a server (HTTPd). The browser evolved into the most popular browser at the time: Netscape Navigator, and the server evolved into the Apache server. Navigator in turn became the basis for Mozilla's Firefox.

At the heart of browsers is a rendering engine. This software takes what comes from servers (HTML, images, audio, video, etc.) and displays the content on the screen. Firefox created what is called the Gecko rendering engine. Apple created WebKit that was initially also used by Google's Chrome. Chrome branched off from that code to create what is now known as Blink. Microsoft originally wrote its own rendering engine but has recently switched to using Blink. While interesting history, an important aspect is that all rendering engines now comply with the World Wide Web Consortium (W3C) standards. The W3C oversees around 40 different standards, including some of the most important ones that we'll be discussing in this book: CSS, the DOM, HTML, SVG, and XML.

Another important standardization body is the European Computer Manufacturers Association (ECMA), now Ecma International. This group creates standards for JavaScript known as ECMAScript (specifically ECMA-262).

Browser Tools

Modern browsers come with a wealth of built-in tools just us, web application developers. This book will be using Chrome throughout this book due to its popularity and availability on all major platforms, but many other browsers have similar functionality. Browsers also have extensions to help with web application development available in their respective stores. We'll keep the set of tools used here to a minimum for ease of installation and use but know that there are many others worth considering.

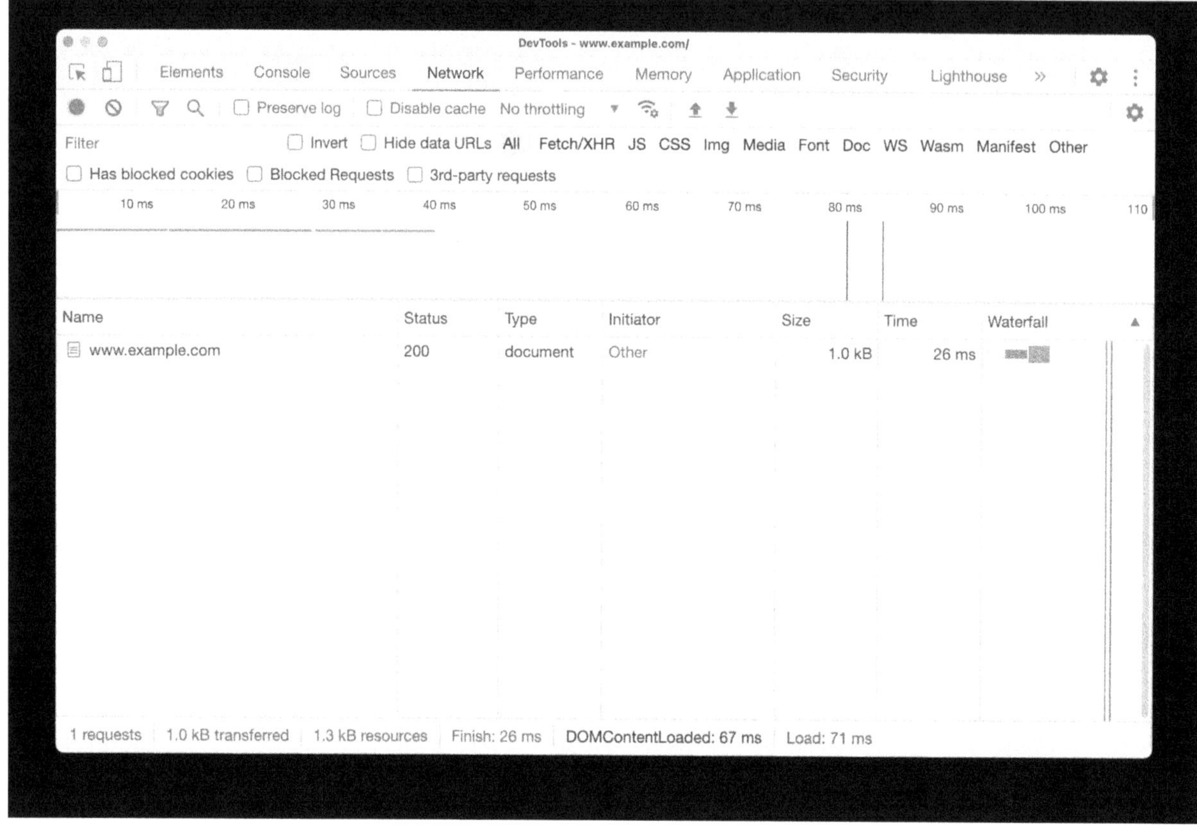

IMG 1.1

Generated with DevTools. Copyright © by Google.

One easy tool available is View Page Source, found via right-clicking (or control-clicking on a Mac) on any tab. One benefit of the web is that much of the underlying HTML etc. content is available to learn from. Chrome's DevTools are found via shift-control-i on Windows and Linux and via option-command-i on Macs, or via the More Tools, Developer Tools menu item.

- In the Elements tab, you can explore the HTML and CSS for the page. You can hover over part of the page and see the HTML and CSS, and hover over the HTML in the Developer Tools page and see where the HTML is on the page. You can also edit the CSS and see how it affects the style of the page.
- The next tab is the Console—an important tool as errors in a page's JavaScript show up here. You can also type in your own JavaScript and see the results.
- The Sources tab shows the various locations of the data displayed on the page and allows you to add your own.
- The Network tab displays where on the web data were loaded and how long each required. This is a great help in finding where network latency slowed down a page load and helps with what to optimize via caching etc.
- The Performance tab extends this by showing how much CPU/GPU/etc. work was required to render the page.

- The Application tab has tools for examining web applications including storage (local, session, web application databases), background services (those scripts running to help an application), caching etc.
- The final tab we'll cover is the Security tab. This covers whether and how the connection is encrypted and whether the web page's certificate is trusted. We'll spend more time later discussing how encryption and security are implemented on the web.

HTTP

The Hypertext Transmission Protocol (HTTP) is an application-layer network protocol. It is very flexible and has subsumed many other application-layer protocols. While it is in its third version, many of the concepts and commands remain unchanged.

Protocols

In government, we have protocol officers who learn, for a particular country, what is acceptable communication and what is not. There are many intricacies of communication in each country or language and what is a compliment in one country or language is an insult in another. To effectively communicate across cultures, we must know how best to express ourselves. The same is true in computer communication. Computers must speak the same language and therefore there are protocol specifications for communication. One of the major protocol specifications for the web is the *Hypertext Transfer Protocol - HTTP/1.1* (https://datatracker.ietf.org/doc/html/rfc2616). RFC stands for Request For Comments, and RFCs are a major way protocols are codified on the internet.

Versions

HTTP has gone through several revisions. HTTP/1.1 was designed to mostly transfer text to share documents. Each request/response cycle is independent of all others. When pages started having richer content (images, audio, video, etc.), this model became somewhat outmoded as a new request/response cycle was needed to fetch each of the elements on a page, even if those elements are coming from the same server. This slows down page loading as there is the TCP/IP connection overhead required to fetch each element (called the three-way handshake).

HTTP/2 added the ability to request to remain connected to a server, at least for a short while, to fetch multiple elements. This is termed pipelining and speeds up page loading. Note, however, that this capability is not used to form sessions where a user authenticates (logs in) to the server; HTTP/2 is an optimization for speed. Authentication typically uses cookies as we'll soon discover. HTTP/2 also added server push such that when a server knows the client will ask for more information (e.g.: a client asks for index.html and that resource references a style.css resource, the server can send style.css without the client requesting it).

HTTP/3 changes the transport mechanism from TCP to a protocol layered on top of the User Datagram Protocol (UDP) named QUIC. HTTP/3 again increases the speed of the web. Importantly, the methods (e.g.: GET), status codes (e.g.: 404), and most headers (e.g.: user-agent) remain unchanged through the three versions.

Requests

Create Read Update Delete (CRUD)

The four most common operations we want to perform on data are the following: to create, read, update, and delete a resource. We call these CRUD and Rails creates everything needed for each of these when it generates a scaffold. As we'll see, we want these operations to be RESTful and Rails provides for this.

Methods

HTTP defines around ten **methods** (sometimes called **verbs**) for requests; we'll be looking at the most used. All request lines have the form `<method> <request-URI> HTTP/<version>`. Uniform Resource Identifiers (URIs) are generally used in the specifications; a Uniform Resource Locator (URL) is a specific type of URI. In either case, it is important to note we talk about resources—those resources may be actual files of course but may also be generated from data on the server in response to requests. The importance of this will become more apparent later when we talk about **Representational State Transfer (REST)**. Note: the method names are in all capitals.

1. **GET** Request a resource from the server. This method is both safe and idempotent. It is considered safe because the resource should not be modified on the server. Idempotent means that no matter how many times the message is sent to the server, the result is always the same (unless something else modifies the resource of course). Idempotency helps with caching—the first response will work for all subsequent requests, allowing any cache between the client and server to respond on behalf of the origin server. We'll discuss caching in **Content Delivery Networks (CDNs)** later; these help with both latency and bandwidth in the web.
2. **HEAD** Request only the header portion of a URI and not the message body. Useful, for example, for checking to see if a large resource has changed since it was last fetched and to use a cached version if the resource hasn't changed. Safe and idempotent.
3. **POST** Add a resource to a collection. In general, the message body becomes a child node of the request URI resource. Neither safe nor idempotent (as multiple POSTs will result in multiple child nodes). POST should be used to create new resources in general.
4. **PUT** Modify (typically replace) a specific resource or create it if it doesn't exist. Different from POST as for a POST the request doesn't specify a specific resource and the contents of the POST are appended, not modified. Idempotent.
5. **PATCH** Modify an existing resource, and usually only certain attributes of that resource, not replace it. Idempotent.
6. **DELETE** Remove the specified resource. Idempotent.

All HTTP requests and responses have the same form: a header with one or more lines, a blank line, and a body. The body is optional for certain types of requests and responses. The blank line is specifically a carriage-return character followed by a line-feed character pair without any preceding text.

Let's first examine simple interactions between a client and a server. We'll use the simplest possible rails server that only serves static content. We can create one of these using the following commands.

Concept Leads to Code

```
rails new Demo
cd Demo
rails server
```

These will be explained in great depth in the coming chapters. For now, it is enough that a web server is running on http://127.0.0.1:3000 and when you point a browser to the URL, it will issue a header with the first line being `GET / HTTP/1.1`. That is, request the "root" document from the server using HTTP version 1.1. After this line, many header lines describe the details of the request. If you are interested in serving simple, static web content, you can place files in the public folder and request them from your client. A quick look at what methods Rails creates for a simple application is illustrative. Run the following five commands.

Concept Leads to Code

```
rails new Todos --minimal
cd Todos
rails generate scaffold Item what:string when:date
rails db:migrate
rails routes
     Prefix Verb   URI Pattern                  Controller#Action
      items GET    /items(.:format)             items#index
            POST   /items(.:format)             items#create
   new_item GET    /items/new(.:format)         items#new
  edit_item GET    /items/:id/edit(.:format)    items#edit
       item GET    /items/:id(.:format)         items#show
            PATCH  /items/:id(.:format)         items#update
            PUT    /items/:id(.:format)         items#update
            DELETE /items/:id(.:format)         items#destroy
rails server
```

While this book will dive deeply into routing, controllers, and actions, we can already see that Rails differentiates actions based on methods (the "Verbs"), and URIs. Depending on what action is desired, a path and method are specified for the resource. You can also specify how you want the results, with the default being an HTML page, but with a JavaScript Object Notation (JSON) result can be automatically created too. This application works: point your browser at http://localhost:3000/items to create a todo list for yourself.

Headers

One of the request header lines describes what the client can accept, based on the Multipurpose Internet Mail Extensions (MIME).

```
Accept: text/html,application/xhtml+xml,application/xml;q=0.9,image/
avif,image/webp,image/apng,*/*;q=0.8
```

These are comma-separated MIME types, with text/html being the first type requested. The q= parameter specifies the quality value that ranks the preference of the various MIME types on a scale from 0 to 1; if q is not specified it is taken to be 1. Note here the client is stating it is willing to accept any MIME type with the specification of */*;q=0.8, though with a lower preference than the other options.

MIME is used to specify content types on the web. It specifies a type and subtype of media. The type is typically text, audio, video, or application. This tells a browser how to display this specific portion of a web resource. text/html is a typical request and response header for HTML resources. There is image/<subtype>, where subtype can be jpeg, gif, png, etc. There is video/<subtype>, where subtype is often mpeg. Similarly, there is audio/<subtype> where subtype here is often mp3. There are many application/<subtype> that are used to invoke programs on the local machine, where subtypes may have values such as javascript, pdf, or vnd.ms-excel (vnd for vendor-specific formats). There is also <octet-stream> that leaves it up to the client to decide how to render the content, based either on the request or the contents of the stream.

Another line states what type of encoding can be accepted; here three different types of compression: Accept-Encoding: gzip, deflate, br.

The following line requests the results in a specific language. Many websites are multi-lingual and will return results based on a client's preference. Here, United States English is specified: Accept-Language: en-US,en;q=0.9.

There are a few caching directives, too many and complex to cover here, but these are relatively self-evident: fetch the resource from the origin instead of any intermediate caches: Cache-Control: no-cache and Pragma: no-cache.

The following line requests that the TCP/IP connection remain open after this request so the client can make multiple requests over the open connection, reducing the amount of time required for subsequent client requests. This is required for HTTP/1.0; persistent, if short-term, connections are the default in HTTP/1.1 and beyond. If the client knows it won't immediately request other resources from the server, it can specify close instead of

keep-alive: Connection: keep-alive

The following line is required starting with HTTP/1.1. The reason this is required is that a single machine (IP address) can host many sites (via virtual hosting) so the client must declare which of the many possible sites it is interested in: Host: localhost:3000.

The User-Agent header specifies who is asking for the resource. Servers can give different results for different clients. Here, the client is a Chrome browser, but the browser states it understands responses Mozilla (Firefox) and Safari in addition to Chrome major version 108: User-Agent: Mozilla/5.0 (Macintosh; Intel Mac OS X 10_15_7) AppleWebKit/537.36 (KHTML, like Gecko) Chrome/108.0.0.0 Safari/537.36.

Certain headers in both requests and responses will begin with X-. These denote extensions that haven't been codified in the HTTP protocol but provide information that may be useful for either side of the transaction.

Body

The body for GET requests is typically empty, but for POSTs and PUTS the body contains the resource information to be created or updated. POSTs should be used to create a new child resource, while PUTs should be used to update a resource if it exists or create a new resource if it doesn't. The POST or PUT body might contain key/value pairs from a form, JSON, a file to be uploaded, etc.

Responses

Responses have a form very similar to requests but with the header starting with: `HTTP/<version> <status code> <message>` The message is optional but useful for humans. For example, `HTTP/1.1 200 OK`. This line is followed by header lines and then a blank line.

Status Codes

Servers respond to the above methods with a variety of status messages. There are five major sets of codes, between 100 and 599. Server responses typically include a short message associated with the status code but are not required to do so. Here is an overview of the typical response codes we see in web applications, but it is not a comprehensive list.

The 100 codes are informational. They do not contain message bodies but signal the client to continue. This might occur if the server can process the overall request, or if the server suggests another approach to transferring data between the client and the server.

The 200 codes are the success message. 200 states that the request was successful. On a GET, the body contains the resources requested. On a HEAD, the response contains only the appropriate header fields. For other methods, the headers and body describe the result of the request. Other 200 messages state that the request was accepted, but that additional may (or may not) be required of the client.

The 300 codes specify redirection: the client must send an additional request to the URI specified. A 301 code states that the resource moved permanently, meaning that subsequent requests should be sent to the new URI specified. It does return the resource on GETs. The new URI will be specified in the Location header, and this response is cacheable as it will never change. The 302 code states that the resource was found and returns the resource on GETs; however, the result is temporary, and the client should continue to use the original URI, contingent on caching headers. The 303 See Other is typically used to redirect the results of a POST to a GET; this allows the results of submitting a form (via a POST) to retrieve the new data (via a GET). The 304 *Not Modified* is an important response code often seen when a conditional GET is sent. This means that the cached copy somewhere in the caching chain is current with the origin resource and so the version in the cache is up to date. The 304 response can dramatically increase the rendering speed for a client.

As a side note, there are strong and weak validators for a resource. Strong validators state the comparison of two different versions of a resource are identical on a bit-by-bit basis. A weak validator states that two resources are semantically equivalent, but possibly not bit-by-bit equivalent. Certain values might be considered "good enough," such as the number of times an article has been read, that fetching the origin value isn't important, or indeed it might be relatively meaningless. Etags sometimes start with a W/ to specify weak validation.

The 400 codes are client errors. The most famous is the 404 *Not Found* of course, but there are others. The 400 *Bad Request* means that the server doesn't understand the syntax of the URI sent in the request. The 401 *Unauthorized* states that the client attempted to access a resource that requires authentication, but that the client hasn't correctly authenticated. 403 *Forbidden* states that the request is understood, but that the server won't permit access for a variety of reasons. The server should state the reason; if it's unwilling to state a reason, it should use a 404 code. 404 *Not Found* covers a wide variety of client errors, most often that the resource specified does not exist on the server. 405 *Method Not Allowed* states that the request method isn't allowed on the resource, although another might be. The 406 *Not Acceptable* states that the resource is available, just not in a form the client has requested in the *Accept* header.

The 500 codes are server errors. The 500 *Internal Server Error* specifies that something caused the server to fail in serving the resource but gives no additional information. These are typically programming errors a software engineer introduced on the server. The 501 *Not Implemented* states that while the server understands the request and the request isn't an error per se, the method isn't implemented for the requested resource.

Headers

One of the lines in the response header is the MIME type of the resource: `Content-Type: text/html; charset=utf-8` This states the response is an HTML web page. Here are two lines about caching: `ETag: W/"95169fc2a0f58a5c49be68df615b2034"` and `Cache-Control: max-age=0, private, must-revalidate`. The first is a weak tag (hash) to the current content, and the second describes the cache control policy.

Cookies

As HTTP was designed as a **stateless** protocol, i.e.: each request and response cycle is independent, something else must be used to create state so we can have sessions, shopping carts, etc. That something else is cookies. Cookies are values shared between servers and clients; the server creates a random value that it stores and then sends that value to the client. The client responds with that value in each request to the server's site and thereby associates itself with a prior request/response. The server now has enough information to continue the conversation even though a persistent connection hasn't occurred. Here is an example of a cookie set by Rails.

```
Set_cookie:
_todos_session=EpzRxj3vV0MNuCluks%2B%2FNInJ4oYreRFbo%2FtxbLyk0IMKF1Kw1igV5y3a
fztOb%2B1133z2Oq%2B%2FIZ3VCaUHzOdspRWH0xOYYSNqwLTTVm%2F5IuG7fTQKwy8J5FUUPKCoW
AeqAEz08aP9jNY4M%2FJ853qQtjvCCwUZx8L6tkWfPs5vA7Sum49rZDINklyHB6Gcmk5nYSdLh0X9
dBVbJIPhscA4ZHHvBnRiIrfBxlQiuA3wIYve%2FgILqZ1oGl4e3fHFDKdJLQPoveOQULwigSxA7qA
lWKp%2FipOtCg%3D%3D--TEykDPqAs5EukirD--mSLASiGeAugVPQqJiSvbIg%3D%3D; path=/;
HttpOnly; SameSite=Lax
```

While this says `_todos_session` it isn't an authenticated session as we'll see in the chapter on security. It does however keep track of further communication from a client as they should now include a `Cookie:` header with the value provided by the `Set_cookie:` from the server. Only those cookies sent by a specific site and path should be returned by the client, and protocol matters: the `HttpOnly;` above denotes that the cookie should only be used with the HTTP protocol, not others such as FTP. When a cookie is delivered by HTTPS, `Secure` is usually also sent to denote that the cookie should only be sent via encrypted communication.

There are many more request and response header lines possible, far too many to describe here. Happily, there are quite a few good web resources that describe them.

Body

The body of the response is the requested resource. This can be HTML, an image, a video, JSON, an application, etc. The browser either displays it if it knows how or starts an external application to deal with the content.

Representational State Transfer (REST)

REST was created to rationalize and normalize interactions between clients and servers, though not necessarily between web clients and servers as the paradigm can be used for any communication. In so doing, REST helps with the scalability of a server and cacheability of resources delivered to a client. In general, a server delivers a resource to a client that both exposes the current state of the resource and the methods available to modify that resource. Rails follows these conventions and is therefore termed RESTful, and in so doing, creates predictable and easy-to-read URLs. REST relies on both the URL and the HTTP verb to map resource interactions. Looking at the above output of `rails routes` we see that reading and posting to the /todos has different actions: the GET verb displays all the current todos and the POST creates a new todo. Similarly, a GET to a single todo results in displaying that one todo, while performing a PUT modifies that todo, and a DELETE removes it. Rails' created HTML views include links as to what operations can be performed on each resource listed.

Content Distribution Networks (CDNs)

As has been said, when a computer is slow, an approach to make it faster is to throw cache at it. This works of course as much of what we do exhibits either temporal or spatial locality. That is, we (or our applications) tend to revisit resources we've visited recently or are in some sense near to what we have visited. So, if we've already downloaded a JavaScript library, image, etc., and our browser has cached it, there is no reason to download that resource again. Note that there are caches in our browsers, often at our organizations and ISPs, and widely distributed throughout the web in CDNs. CDNs cache web resources closer (typically this means fewer network hops, but by some metric faster) than the origin resource. They typically work by intercepting calls to resources via the Domain Name System (DNS) and directing specific requests to a closer server. Organizations typically pay for a CDN to distribute their resources as these caches provide a faster, and therefore more compelling experience to their users. REST, and therefore Rails, creates resources and routes that play well with CDNs and will therefore create better interactions with users.

Summary

We've covered a lot of important background information in this chapter, all of which we'll be using for the rest of the book. It is critical to understand all of this to become a successful web application developer. First, we looked at the creation and development of the web—why it was created, how it leveraged existing work, and how it adapted to changes in computing and society. We then looked at the tools built into our browsers that most people won't need but a crucial to developers. We need to know what our browsers don't understand by looking at the console. We need to know where the performance bottlenecks occur—is it in the server, the network, or the additional parts downloaded from the web—and what do we need to cache to increase an application's performance? These data can be found in the network, performance, and memory tabs. We then plumbed the depths of the basic web protocol, HTTP. Much of the initial protocol remains in place, including the original commands (verbs) and responses (100–500 codes). Recent versions have responded to the need and ability to increase the speed and therefore the responsiveness and useability of applications.

We then spent some time looking at the messages sent using HTTP. There are requests and responses and from a high-level point of view, they look similar. A request message (verb) line or a response line with an associated numeric result code. Both are then followed by header lines that give more detail to the request or response, then a blank line, and finally a body to the message if appropriate.

Exercises

Directions: Use what you learned in this chapter to complete the following tasks and exercises.

1. Visit `https://example.com`, view the page source, and examine its various aspects with the developer tools. What takes the longest to load? Are any of the data cached?
2. Type `console.log ("Hello, world!");` in the console tab and explain what it does.
3. Go to several of your favorite websites and look for errors in the console tab, see the performance in the network and performance tabs, and check their security in the security tab.
4. There are many non-browser tools that can use to interact with websites. Curl (https://curl.se/), wget (https://www.gnu.org/software/wget/), and Postman (https://www.postman.com/) are three examples. Download one or more and use them to explore a website.
5. Surf to the Wayback Machine (https://archive.org/web/) and follow the evolution of one of your favorite websites through the years.

CHAPTER 2

Ruby for Rails

> *"Ruby is an interpreted, high-level, general-purpose programming language which supports multiple programming paradigms. It was designed with an emphasis on programming productivity and simplicity. In Ruby, everything is an object, including primitive data types. It was developed in the mid-1990s by Yukihiro "Matz" Matsumoto in Japan.*
> *Ruby is dynamically typed and uses garbage collection and just-in-time compilation. It supports multiple programming paradigms, including procedural, object-oriented, and functional programming."*
>
> https://en.wikipedia.org/wiki/Ruby_(programming_language)
> retrieved 2023-01-17

Introduction

While Ruby has many of the features of other object-oriented programming (OOP) languages, it expresses some of those features differently and it has some features that don't exist in many other languages. It allows for the expression of complicated ideas succinctly. This is one of its great benefits as fewer lines written leads to fewer bugs written. And as with all languages, there are Ruby (and therefore Rails) idioms that need to be covered before starting our exploration of Rails.

Learning Outcomes

By the end of this chapter, you'll be able to do the following:

1. Create programs that leverage the big four OOP principles, leading to better-designed and -architected applications.
2. Use object-oriented techniques to create appropriate APIs for all your classes by using encapsulation to hide details other classes don't need to know and using the correct visibility to allow for appropriate extension. Every class we write has an API, and getting this right the first time makes the use and maintenance much easier.
3. Use the strengths of Ruby to create readable, parsimonious programs and apply that knowledge to other programming languages. It is important to understand that all programming languages are created to solve specific problems and are created in a specific environment. They are all opinionated, and knowing how those opinions differ leads us to be stronger programmers.

Key Terms

The following important **terms** will be introduced in this chapter.

- **Abstraction**
- **Encapsulation**
- **Inheritance**
- **Polymorphism**
- **Dynamic arrays**
- **Dictionaries**
- **Symbols**
- **Scopes**

Object-Oriented Programming (OOP)

OOP is an attempt to address the biggest issue in modern program development: complexity. We are no longer able to deal with the complexity of even simple programs, let alone the millions of lines of code that make up typical applications. It is an actual physical limitation our species has: we can't deal with more than seven (plus or minus two) in our working memory, source http://psychclassics.yorku.ca/Miller/ and https://en.wikipedia.org/wiki/The_Magical_Number_Seven,_Plus_or_Minus_Two. In computing this means that when there are more than seven variables, nesting levels, etc., not only do we not understand the program, we simply cannot. When programs are small, say less than several thousand lines of code, we might be able to understand much of what they do. Beyond this (i.e., when programs become interesting) we can't have that understanding. However, we can understand small parts of them at a time. So, the problem becomes narrowing our focus to contain seven or fewer items in our short-term, working, memory. This leads to the need to abstract away from many of the details we are constantly working with, to look at problems at a higher level of abstraction.

Many point to Simula 67 as the forerunner to OOP as it "...introduced objects, classes, inheritance and subclasses, virtual procedures, coroutines, and discrete event simulation, and featured garbage collection." Source: https://en.wikipedia.org/wiki/Simula. Simula 67 inspired Smalltalk, which in turn was part of the inspiration for Ruby.

OOP's basis is independent objects, each holding state and communicating with others. State here means what an object currently represents, and we think of this as the values its variables hold. Objects expose the services they can provide to other objects via visible (public) messages that can be sent to them. We tend to call these messages methods and while we'll follow this convention, thinking about objects and the messages one can send them is often the more useful paradigm.

To create a new object, there is a blueprint, a design, that the object is based upon. These are called classes or prototypes. We typically instantiate a new object with a certain initial state via calling a "new" method.

The Big Four of OOP

Object-Oriented Programming languages (OOP) are typically defined by four major attributes. You can use the mnemonic of the vowels (and of course an off-by-one error) to remember them. They are A, E, I, and O+1.

Abstraction

The A is **abstraction**, and this may well be the most important. We need to abstract away from the details of the data we are using as we are often dealing with more data than we can deal with. In the end, of course, all data are represented in a binary form in the computer, but few of us think in binary on an ongoing basis. We think in terms of higher-level abstractions. We think in terms of combinations of strings and numbers. Indeed, much if not all of what we store are combinations of strings and numbers. It can be argued of course that everything is a binary (numeric) value, including characters and therefore strings.

- Boolean values are one-bit numbers.
- Integers, decimal, and floating-point numbers are usually represented directly in an underlying machine representation.
- Dates are multiple numbers.
- Images are carefully specified files of numbers.
- Audio and video files are numbers that represent sounds and video frames.
- Phone and identification numbers might either be numbers or strings and might move between the two as needed.

While all this is true, we'd like to not care how a date is stored. For example, is the day, month, or year the first value in a date? We should not have to think about these details, we simply want to perform date arithmetic without knowing how it occurs. We want to know that invalid dates, leap seconds, years, etc., are all dealt with correctly so we can create applications assuming those are correct. When an object provides services and we can count on those services remaining correct, regardless of whether the underlying data or algorithms change, we can abstract away from (essentially ignore) the implementation. We want services that work, we don't want to know how they work. The same must be true for those objects we create that provide services to other objects of course. Each time we create a class, we create an Application Programming Interface (API) for it with the visible elements. It's important to keep the API as constant as possible so that clients of our classes know what to expect in terms of functionality.

Ruby has many of the usual Abstract Data Types (ADTs) but several behave somewhat differently than in other languages.

Arrays

For example, arrays in Ruby are a little different than in most languages. They store values of any type, though this isn't a surprise as there is only one type in Ruby: references to objects. Thus, while they appear to be heterogeneous, the beauty and consistency of a truly object-oriented programming language shine here. Arrays in other languages tend to have a set size; this is not true in Ruby. Ruby arrays are dynamically sized in response to adding and removing values. Any gaps that may form by doing so are filled with `nils`. Ruby arrays are 0-based; negative numbers can be used to index from the end instead of the beginning of the array. Slices can be taken using indices or ranges.

Arrays in Ruby have many unconventional operations. There are set `intersection`, `difference`, and `union`. There also are `push`, `pop`, `shift`, and `unshift` for treating an array like a queue or deque.

There are many methods mixed in from enumerable: `collect` (map), `each`, `find`, `find_all` (select), `grep`, and `sort`. Most of these can take a block to execute giving us much of the same functionality as traditional functional programming languages. Here are some examples that demonstrate some of the interesting aspects of Ruby's arrays. Note that there are return values for almost all Ruby statements including assignment. In Ruby, almost everything is an expression whose result can be used in another expression. This adds to the power and flexibility of Ruby. In many languages, assignment returns a value (the assignment of a variable often being a side effect) so that statements such as `A = B = C = 42` work.

Concept Leads to Code

```
irb
# regular expressions are objects
irb> a = [/regex/]
=> [/regex/]
irb> a[5] = "foo"
=> "foo"
irb> a
=> [/regex/, nil, nil, nil, nil, "foo"]
irb> a.pop
=> "foo"
irb> a
=> [/regex/, nil, nil, nil, nil]
irb> a.compact
=> [/regex/]
irb> b = (0..5).to_a
=> [0, 1, 2, 3, 4, 5]
irb> b.map{|i| i*i}
=> [0, 1, 4, 9, 16, 25]
irb> b.filter{|i| i > 3}
=> [4, 5]
irb> c.reduce(:+)
=> 15
irb> c = (0..5).to_a
=> [0, 1, 2, 3, 4, 5]
irb> d = (4..10).to_a
=> [4, 5, 6, 7, 8, 9, 10]
irb> c.union(d)
=> [0, 1, 2, 3, 4, 5, 6, 7, 8, 9, 10]
irb> c.intersection(d)
=> [4, 5]
irb> c.difference(d)
=> [0, 1, 2, 3]
irb> c[-1]
=> 5
irb> c[3,2]
=> [3, 4]
irb> d[2..3]
=> [6, 7]
```

Symbols

Ruby symbols begin with a `:` sigil. This creates a global identifier, not a variable, though it is an object. We cannot assign to nor change a symbol once created. They are added to a global set named Symbol. In other languages, Ruby's symbols can be thought of as a dynamic global enumeration. Rails uses symbols extensively to specify values passed as parameters.

Hashes

Ruby's hashes are similar to other languages and are sometimes called **dictionaries** or associative arrays in those languages. These are what we call key/value pairs. The values are accessed by indexing via the key;

keys must be unique while values don't need to be. If a key is added more than once, the most recent value overwrites the existing one. As both keys and values are references to objects, so long as an object has a hash method it can be used as a key. Unusually, this includes `nils` and regular expressions.

The general format for hash literals is curly brackets, with keys and values separated with '=>'. Key/value pairs are separated with commas. If the key is a symbol, you can use '`symbol:`' instead of '`:symbol =>`'.

Hashes have the same enumerable mixin as arrays and so have access to all those methods. Hashes have an index method that returns the key for a given value. Hashes also have methods to return an array of all the keys or all the values.

Concept Leads to Code

```
irb
irb> a = {"a" => "b"}
=> {"a"=>"b"}
irb> a = {:a => "b"}
=> {:a=>"b"}
irb> a = {a: "b"}
=> {:a=>"b"}
irb> a = {1 => "one"}
=> {1=>"one"}
irb> a = {/regex/ => "regex"}
=> {/regex/=>"regex"}
irb> a = {nil => "nil"}
=> {nil=>"nil"}
irb> a = {a: "eh", b: "bee", c: "see"}
=> {:a=>"eh", :b=>"bee", :c=>"see"}
irb> a.map{|i| i}
=> [[:a, "eh"], [:b, "bee"], [:c, "see"]]
irb> a[:a]
=> "eh"
```

Encapsulation

The E is **encapsulation**, a technique that helps with abstraction, and dealing with complexity in general. Many years ago, control flow was what we now consider unstructured. That is, the now-common loops and control structures were not in wide use. Indeed, Dijkstra wrote a paper in 1968 pointing out that unstructured programs are difficult to understand and maintain. It is entitled *Go To Statement Considered Harmful* source: https://homepages.cwi.nl/~storm/teaching/reader/Dijkstra68.pdf (retrieved 2023-01-16).

While structured programming became standard relatively quickly, structured data has taken longer to become commonplace. In general, many languages and frameworks continue to support and indeed encourage shared mutable data. Shared mutable data are the "goto"s of the data world. We cannot count on any value we have a reference to as it may be changed by another object that has similar access. This is to say nothing of the difficulties of creating thread-safe programs in the face of shared mutable data creating critical sections.

Encapsulation can help with this when used wisely. Objects should hide as much as possible about their implementation. The use of public, protected, and private data and methods is a major approach to encapsulation.

We shouldn't care how an object implements its behavior. It could be that when a datum is requested the object calculates the value each time. Or it could be that the datum is a fixed value that is returned. Or it is calculated once and cached. We shouldn't care: we want the service and shouldn't have to think about how it is provided. This is termed referential transparency: that a calculated value can be replaced with a constant, and vice versa. We also shouldn't have to care when the implementation changes. The algorithm and underlying data representation can (and will) change, but if the interface remains the same, the clients won't notice the difference.

An object shouldn't change behavior during its lifetime. If you need a different behavior, you should create a new object. While it has been argued that this is inefficient, the speed at which new objects are created and old objects are garbage collected these days is essentially instantaneous. We need to move from concern about how fast a program is to how best to support humans in developing, testing, deploying, and maintaining programs as this is where almost all problems now exist.

Here are a few good rules of thumb to aid in encapsulation.

1. All class and instance variables should be private or protected. None should be directly writable by another object. Objects that use the API of an object should not care how the services are provided, nor the internal state of an object.
2. Most if not all methods should refer to one or more class or instance variables. If a method does not, why is it in this class? Might it be better to have it in a mixin, or not have it at all? We use the term highly coherent to denote classes where all the data and methods are related to each other, and classes are typically easier to understand if they are highly coherent.
3. A related concept is loosely coupled meaning that one class isn't tightly tied to the implementation of another class. Classes that are encapsulated help with this.
4. All accessors should be read-only and there should be no mutators.

Scopes and Sigils

Scope is a major aspect of encapsulation—where a variable or method is visible (specifically: modifiable) dramatically affects how well a program can hide its implementation. Ruby takes an approach different from many other languages by using *sigils* to specify the scope for most variables. Other languages use blocks to encapsulate variables, typically inside of classes and methods. Ruby does follow this for local variables, but for globals, class, instance variables, and symbols, Ruby prefixes the variable with either `$` for globals, `@@` for class, `@` for instance variables, and `:` for symbols. These can be specified pretty much anywhere; for example, a global can be created inside a class method. Class and instance variables are private by default, with methods being public by default. Ruby does have the ability to change class methods visibility to `public`, `private`, and `protected`, and instance variable visibility with `attr_reader`, `attr_writer`, and `attr_accessor`.

Concept Leads to Code

```
# Demonstrate the visibility of various types of variable,
# both in a class and outside of one.
$global = "global"

local = "local"
SCOPES = ["$global", "local", "method_local", "@@class", "@instance"]

class Demo
  @@class = "class"

  def initialize
    @instance = "instance"
  end

  def scope
    method_local = "method"

    SCOPES.each do |n|
      begin
        puts(eval(n))        # eval shouldn't usually be used
      rescue NameError
        # normally, don't leave this empty
      end
    end
  end
end

demo = Demo.new
demo.scope
puts "----"
SCOPES.each do |n|
  begin
    puts(eval(n))        # eval shouldn't usually be used
  rescue
    # normally, don't leave this empty
  end
end

# Output:
global
method
class
instance
----
global
local
```

Inheritance

The I of the vowels is **inheritance**. As in life, classes can inherit something without earning it. That is, a (child or derived) class can gain functionality from a base (parent or super) class's implementation. When a class extends another, it has access to all the public and protected members (data and methods) of the base class.

Inheritance should be used with caution as it is less flexible than referencing. Make sure a class is-a base class and doesn't simply a *has-a* relationship. Of course, there are times when a child class has all the attributes of a parent class. A cat is a mammal is an animal, so this derivation makes sense. A sorted list on the other hand might not have all the properties of a generic list. For example, a pop from a sorted list will return the largest value of the list, while a pop from a generic list will return the last item added. Here, the semantics are quite different, and a sorted list should probably have a generic list but isn't a generic list, so should refer to a list but not inherit from one.

Some languages (e.g.: Python, C++) allow a class to inherit from multiple base classes, while others (Java, Ruby) allow a class to inherit from only one class. This is termed *single inheritance*. It limits a certain amount of flexibility, but Ruby also allows for *mixins*—another way of gaining functionality without having to write it. Single inheritance is also easier to understand than *multiple inheritance* and this simplification is a major reason many languages choose it.

For Ruby, the < character is used to express the extension of a base class; other languages might use the `extends` keyword. The following example also demonstrates the `method_missing` method in Ruby that is used in Rails. It is automatically called on an object when a matching method isn't found, and it can respond directly or create a new method associated with the object.

Concept Leads to Code

```
class Animal
  # https://en.wikipedia.org/wiki/Animal
  TRAITS = ["eat", "breathe", "move", "reproduce"]

  def method_missing(m, *args, &block)
    TRAITS.include?("#{m}".sub(/\?/, ""))
  end
end

class Mammal < Animal
  # https://en.wikipedia.org/wiki/Mammal
  TRAITS = ["fur", "hair", "lactate"]

  def method_missing(m, *args, &block)
    if TRAITS.include?("#{m}".sub(/\?/, ""))
      true
    else
      super(m, *args, &block)
    end
  end
end

class Cat < Mammal
  # https://en.wikipedia.org/wiki/Cat
```

```
  TRAITS = ["claws", "sharp_teeth"]

  def method_missing(m, *args, &block)
    if TRAITS.include?("#{m}".sub(/\?/, ""))
      true
    else
      super(m, *args, &block)
    end
  end
end

animal = Animal.new
p animal.eat?
p animal.claws?

cat = Cat.new
p cat.eat?
p cat.fur?
p cat.claws?

# Output
true
false
true
true
true
```

Mixins are defined using the `module` declaration. There is only one instance of a module visible at any point in the program.

Concept Leads to Code

```
# Uses only parameters, no need for class
module Conversions
  @@F2C = 5/9.0
  @@C2F = 9/5.0

  def c2f(celcius)
    (celcius * @@C2F) + 32
  end

  def f2c(fahrenheit)
    (fahrenheit - 32) * @@F2C
  end
end

include Conversions
p f2c(212)
p c2f(100)

module Instantiate
  attr_reader :var
  def init(i)
    @var = i        # modules can have variables
  end
end

include Instantiate
init(42)
p var

# most recent definition is used
module One
  def definition
    "first definition"
  end
end

module Two
  def definition
    "second definition"
  end
end

include One
include Two
p definition

# Output
100.0
212.0
42
"second definition"
```

Polymorphism

The 0+1 P is **polymorphism**. We often have off-by-one errors in our code as arrays tend to be 0-based in our programming languages (including Ruby). The first element in an array is element 0 and this fact has led to all kinds of issues in programs. That said, polymorphism is from the Greek language and means “many shapes.” In OOP, this denotes methods that can take different types of arguments and perform the same operations on them. A Ruby example is the sort method on an array. We can sort both strings and integers, and we can specify (inject) a method to do the comparisons that works for both strings and integers, allowing us to sort heterogeneous arrays.

Concept Leads to Code

```
irb
irb> ["5", "2", "1"].sort
=> ["1", "2", "5"]
irb> [5, 2, 1].sort
=> [1, 2, 5]
irb> arr = ['5', 1, '2', 4, 3]
=> ["5", 1, "2", 4, 3]
irb> arr.sort{ |x, y| x.to_i  y.to_i }
=> [1, "2", 3, 4, "5"]
```

Debugging

We all write bugs: errors in our programs. There are many reasons for this, chief among them the complexities of the applications we are creating. We must become experts at debugging our applications including examining the developer console of our browser, the logs of our server, and interacting directly with a running application. Rails has a built-in debugging shell that lets us directly query and modify the current state of an application. It is activated by the gem debug in the `Gemfile`. The usual Ruby debug functionality (https://github.com/ruby/debug) is available. An easy way to activate the debugger is to simply call the `debugger` method in a file where we need to examine the data for an error. The following commands and others are then available to us.

- break
  - List all the current breakpoints.
  - N: set a breakpoint in the current file at line number N.
  - F:N: set a breakpoint in file F at line number N.
  - C#M: set a breakpoint in class C at method M.
- delete
  - Delete all or a specific breakpoint number.
- info
  - Show the relevant Rails variables.
- step
  - Step into the next line; if it is a function call, step into the function.

- next
  - Go to the next line; if it is a function call, do not step into the function.
- continue
  - Resume the running of the Rails application until the next breakpoint, if there is one.

Let's say we added a `priority` field in the object without remembering to add it to the `item_params` method of the controller. We can put a `debugger` statement in the controller to see what is going on.

Concept Leads to Code

```
Started POST "/items" for 127.0.0.1 at 2024-02-21 07:59:53 -0700
Processing by ItemsController#create as HTML
  Parameters: {"authenticity_token"=>"[FILTERED]", "item"=>{"what"=>"Melissa
Cordova", "when"=>"2024-02-21", "priority"=>"5"}, "commit"=>"Create Item"}
[19, 28] in /private/tmp/Todo/app/controllers/items_controller.rb
    19|   def edit
    20|   end
    21|
    22|   # POST /items
    23|   def create
=>  24|     debugger
    25|     @item = Item.new(item_params)
    26|
    27|     if @item.save
    28|       redirect_to @item, notice: "Item was successfully created."
=>#0        ItemsController#create at /private/tmp/Todo/app/controllers/
items_controller.rb:24
  #1        ActionController::BasicImplicitRender#send_action(method="create",
args=[]) at ~/.rbenv/versions/3.1.2/lib/ruby/gems/3.1.0/gems/actionpack-7.0.8/
lib/action_controller/metal/basic_implicit_render.rb:6
  # and 66 frames (use `bt' command for all frames)
# Call item_params to see what is wrong.
(rdbg) p item_params
Unpermitted parameter: :priority. Context: { controller: ItemsController,
action: create, request: #, params: {"authenticity_token"=>"[FILTERED]",
"item"=>{"what"=>"Melissa Cordova", "when"=>"2024-02-21", "priority"=>"5"},
"commit"=>"Create Item", "controller"=>"items", "action"=>"create"} }
# Okay, we didn't allow priority in so it's not set.
(rdbg) p @item
=> #
# Let's set it here.
(ruby) @item.priority=5
5
# Looks better.
(rdbg) p @item
=> #
# Continue running the server with a better version of the object.
(rdbg) c
  TRANSACTION (0.0ms)  begin transaction
  ↳ app/controllers/items_controller.rb:27:in `create'
  Item Create (1.0ms)  INSERT INTO "items" ("what", "when", "created_at",
"updated_at", "priority") VALUES (?, ?, ?, ?, ?)  [["what", "Melissa Cordova"],
["when", "2024-02-21"], ["created_at", "2024-02-21 15:16:27.533377"],
["updated_at", "2024-02-21 15:16:27.533377"], ["priority", 5]]
  ↳ app/controllers/items_controller.rb:27:in `create'
  TRANSACTION (0.9ms)  commit transaction
  ↳ app/controllers/items_controller.rb:27:in `create'
Redirected to http://localhost:3000/items/3
Completed 302 Found in 994410ms (ActiveRecord: 2.3ms | Allocations: 514048)
```

Summary

We've looked at Ruby through the lens of OOP. We've learned what the big four of OOP are and how Ruby expresses each. Ruby has some interesting features such as **dynamic arrays** and **symbols**, both of which we'll see used in the coming chapters. We're now ready to dive into creating web applications!

Exercises

Directions: Use what you learned in this chapter to complete the following tasks and exercises.

1. We use object abstractions all the time in real life. Most of us don't know the internal workings of the cars, buses, motorcycles, planes, etc., we use for transportation. We know the parts we can see, but not how all the engines, motors, etc. interact. Create an API that has both public and private methods associated with some form of transportation.
2. Calendars encapsulate many different rules that we as users aren't typically aware of. For example, leap years (those with an additional day in February) occur every four years unless the year is divisible by 100 and not divisible by 400. The dates for national holidays, election days, etc. also vary from year to year. Design a class with public and private methods to model these differences. Consider what information a client of your class needs to know.
3. Life has long been divided into trees using the characteristics of living things. The Linnaean Taxonomy (https://en.wikipedia.org/wiki/Linnaean_taxonomy) was first published in 1735 and creates a tree to represent the relationships between species. Much has been learned since then of course, but it was a good early attempt. Model part of the Linnaean taxonomy using Ruby's inheritance. Consider what characteristics (attributes) are common to a species and which aren't when forming your tree.
4. Ruby doesn't in general allow operations between integers and strings. While 3.to_s returns `"3"`, any `string.to_i` returns `0`. Extend the String and Integer classes to allow certain operations to occur between them, i.e.: make them more polymorphic. An example would be allowing `3*"foo"` to produce `"foofoofoo"`. You'll need to define the semantics of each operation. Note that, in general, extending a preexisting API should be approached with a great deal of caution.

CHAPTER 3

Models

"I found myself answering the same questions asked frequently of me by different people. It would be so much easier if everyone could just read my database."

Tim Berners-Lee

"Data dominates. If you've chosen the right data structures and organized things well, the algorithms will almost always be self-evident. Data structures, not algorithms, are central to programming."

Rob Pike

"Bad programmers worry about the code. Good programmers worry about data structures and their relationships"

Linus Torvalds

Introduction

All computers do just two things: transform and possibly display data. It is their ability to do so quickly and accurately that drives the development of software. The web makes all this accessible to almost everyone. In this chapter, we will discuss data representations and how data are structured in relationship with each other. This is one of the most crucial tasks as there are subtle interactions between data that we must capture, and it is rarely obvious how to model the data. For example, how many phones should a person be allowed to have? What happens to the phones when the person moves carriers? Should they be assigned to no one? Should they have to be reconfigured to the new carrier? What if one or more are business phones and the person takes another job? Getting these details correct not only simplifies our databases, they lead to what is called the Principle Of Least Astonishment (POLA) for users of our applications.

Learning Outcomes

By the end of this chapter, you'll be able to do the following.

1. Use Rails' conventions so that very little configuration needs to be done to quickly have a fully working web application.
2. Utilize the active record paradigm in a Rails application.
3. Build one-to-one, one-to-many, and many-to-many relationships in a relational database system.
4. Use embedding in your application to use a non-relational database system.

5. Use test-driven development for all your application development.
6. Create model validations to assure data cleanliness.

Key Terms

The following important **terms** will be introduced in this chapter.

- **Model—View—Controller**
- **Relational database systems**
- **Normalization**
- **Non-relational database systems**
- **Primary key**
- **Foreign key**
- **Object-Relational Mapping**
- **Object-Document Mapping**
- **Test-Driven Development**
- **Validations**

Databases

There are many different types of databases, from simple flat files to massive geographically distributed databases with concurrent access. We'll keep things relatively simple here, using SQLite (https://www.sqlite.org/) as this is the default for Rails, and MongoDB (https://www.mongodb.com/) as an example of a **non-relational database**. For **relational databases**, Rails provides a flexible Object-Relational Mapper (ORM) that can connect to a variety of databases. There are also several Object-Document Mappers for non-relational databases such as MongoDB.

We'll use SQLite for most examples as it does not require credential management and is very widely deployed. According to the website, every

- Android device,
- iPhone and iOS devices,
- Mac,
- Windows machine,
- Firefox, Chrome, and Safari web browsers,

and many other devices and applications have SQLite built in.

For relational databases, Rails provides commands to create, manage, delete, etc. databases. Relational databases have a schema to describe the tables and the contents of those tables. In Rails, the current schema is found in `db/schema.rb`. Non-relational databases, due to their not having schema, typically require somewhat less management.

First, for any relational database, we need to create an empty database instance and Rails has the **`rails db:create`** command. This creates the database that will be used for an application and relies on the configuration in `config/database.yml` for the information about the database used. The `rails new` commands typically specify the type of database such as **`rails -d postgresql or rails -d mysql`**; if we don't specify, we get SQLite. To examine the current contents of a SQLite database, we can use **`sqlite3 -list db/development.sqlite3 .dump`** or **`sqlite3 -list storage/development.sqlite3 .dump`** depending on the version of Rails we are using. Of course, we can change databases at any time, making sure we migrate the existing data to the new database. In an existing Rails directory, we can run the command **`rails –tasks`** to see the current set of options we have available. Looking at the `db` set, the most important database management commands are the following.

- `rails db:create`
  - Create the databases specified in `config/database.yml`. This typically includes the development, testing, and production databases.
- `rails db:drop`
  - Remove all the current databases, removing all their data. Again, this typically includes the development, testing, and production databases. While useful during development, be very careful about losing data in a production environment.
- `rails db:migrate`
  - Add/remove/modify the database schema, see below.
- `rails db:reset`
  - Run rails `db:drop` and then rails `db:create`.
- `rails db:rollback`
  - Revert to the most recent modification to the schema.

Once a database is created, we need to manage the tables and their relationships in the schema file. Rails manages changes to the schema via *migrations*.

Migrations

Changes to the current database schema (the tables, rows, and columns) are managed by Ruby files called migrations. They migrate the schema from one version to another.
When we are creating database entries, Rails recognizes the following types (https://guides.rubyonrails.org/v3.2.21/migrations.html#supported-types).

- binary
- boolean
- date
- datetime
- decimal
- float
- integer
- primary_key
- references

- string
- text
- time
- timestamp

String is the default. The `references` is an important type as it is a **foreign key** that references a **primary key** in another table. This is a reference in OO terminology. It turns into an integer in the database, and that is appropriate as it is the primary key in the other table.

The general methods available for migrations are as follows.

- add_column
- add_index
- add_timestamps
- change_column
- change_table
- create_table
- drop_table
- remove_column
- remove_index
- remove_timestamps
- rename_column
- rename_index
- rename_table

Several generators automatically create migrations, including `scaffold`, `model`, and of course `migration`.

Concept Leads to Code

```
rails generate scaffold Item what when:date
# db/migrate/20240228120745_create_items.rb
class CreateItems < ActiveRecord::Migration[7.1]
  def change
    create_table :items do |t|
      t.string :what
      t.date :when


      t.timestamps
    end
  end
end
rails db:migrate
== 20240307121535 CreateItems: migrating
======================================
-- create_table(:items)
   -> 0.0008s
== 20240307121535 CreateItems: migrated (0.0008s)
=============================
# db/schema.rb
ActiveRecord::Schema[7.1].define(version: 2024_02_28_120745) do
  create_table "items", force: :cascade do |t|
    t.string "what"
    t.date "when"
    t.datetime "created_at", null: false
    t.datetime "updated_at", null: false
  end
end
sqlite3 -list storage/development.sqlite3 .dump
CREATE TABLE IF NOT EXISTS "schema_migrations" ("version" varchar NOT NULL
PRIMARY KEY);
INSERT INTO schema_migrations VALUES('20240307121535');
CREATE TABLE IF NOT EXISTS "items" ("id" integer PRIMARY KEY AUTOINCREMENT NOT
NULL, "what" varchar, "when" date, "created_at" datetime(6) NOT NULL,
"updated_at" datetime(6) NOT NULL);CREATE TABLE IF NOT EXISTS
"schema_migrations" ("version" varchar NOT NULL PRIMARY KEY);
```

We'll be using two major migration methods, AddXtoY and RemoveXFromY. In both cases, the X does not particularly matter, other than for documentation purposes. Also in both cases, the Y matters a lot as it specifies the table columns are added or removed. Each must also have column names and types we are specifically interested in adding or removing as with the Create above. All migration files start with a timestamp in the form of YYYYMMDDHHMMSS and are recorded in the database. Here is how we can add a column to a database.

Concept Leads to Code

```
rails generate migration AddPriorityToItem priority:integer
# 20240228121600_add_priority_to_item.rb
class AddPriorityToItem < ActiveRecord::Migration[7.1]
  def change
    add_column :items, :priority, :integer
  end
end
# rails db:migrate
# db/schema.rb
ActiveRecord::Schema[7.1].define(version: 2024_02_28_121951) do
  create_table "items", force: :cascade do |t|
    t.string "what"
    t.date "when"
    t.datetime "created_at", null: false
    t.datetime "updated_at", null: false
    t.integer "priority"
  end
end
sqlite3 -list storage/development.sqlite3 .dump
CREATE TABLE IF NOT EXISTS "items" ("id" integer PRIMARY KEY AUTOINCREMENT NOT
NULL, "what" varchar, "when" date, "created_at" datetime(6) NOT NULL,
"updated_at" datetime(6) NOT NULL, "priority" integer);
```

Of course, when we add columns to a database, we must add to the views and controllers to reflect these changes. The same for when we remove/modify columns. We can add multiple data in the same migration.

Concept Leads to Code

```
rails generate migration AddStuffToItem one two
# 20240228121737_add_stuff_to_item.rb
class AddStuffToItem < ActiveRecord::Migration[7.1]
  def change
    add_column :items, :one, :string
    add_column :items, :two, :string
  end
end
# db/schema.rb
ActiveRecord::Schema[7.1].define(version: 2024_02_28_121737) do
  create_table "items", force: :cascade do |t|
    t.string "what"
    t.date "when"
    t.datetime "created_at", null: false
    t.datetime "updated_at", null: false
    t.integer "priority"
    t.string "one"
    t.string "two"
  end
end
sqlite3 -list storage/development.sqlite3 .dump
CREATE TABLE IF NOT EXISTS "items" ("id" integer PRIMARY KEY AUTOINCREMENT NOT
NULL, "what" varchar, "when" date, "created_at" datetime(6) NOT NULL,
"updated_at" datetime(6) NOT NULL, "priority" integer, "one" varchar, "two"
varchar);
```

We can also remove columns using a migration. Here's an example that removes the two we just added.

Concept Leads to Code

```
rails generate migration RemoveStuffFromItem one two
# 20240228121951_remove_stuff_from_item.rb
class RemoveStuffFromItem < ActiveRecord::Migration[7.1]
  def change
    remove_column :items, :one, :string
    remove_column :items, :two, :string
  end
end
```

Another, and possibly cleaner approach is to roll back the most recent modifications. Once we roll back a modification, we should delete the migration (file) that created it so that it won't be run in the future. Rails knows enough about migrations to reverse the action of many changes without us having to specify them.

Concept Leads to Code

```
rails db:rollback
== 20240307025143 AddStuffToItem: reverting
====================================
-- remove_column(:items, :two, :string)
   -> 0.0047s
-- remove_column(:items, :one, :string)
   -> 0.0037s
== 20240307025143 AddStuffToItem: reverted (0.0110s)
==========================
```

MVC

There are many different types of architectures for applications, but the dominant one for interactive applications is called **Model, View, and Controller (MVC)**. It was created by Trygve Reenskaug while working on a Smalltalk environment at the Xerox Palo Alto Research Center in the 1970s. Smalltalk had a strong influence on many of the OO languages that came after it, including Ruby. One of the reasons MVC became so popular is what is termed the *separation of concerns*. That is, we have several different concerns when developing an application such as the following.

1. What the data are and how they are stored (persistence).
2. What the user interface looks like and how it behaves.
3. What is unique about this application, i.e., the logic behind it.

These are the three parts of MVC. The model is typically some form of database, such as a relational (often called an *"SQL"*) database or a non-relational (often called a *"No-SQL"*) database. These have a language unto themselves, as do the views and controllers. The views for web applications are typically in one of two forms: HTML or JSON. Rails by default creates both when a view is generated, and others can be added via gems. Controllers in Rails are written in Ruby of course. Indeed, Rails provides Ruby interfaces to the model and views too, allowing us to mostly stay in one language and avoid "context switching"—switching between different languages and paradigms—increasing our effectiveness when developing an application. The Ruby interface to the model is called an **Object-Relational Mapping (ORM)** for relational databases, or an **Object-Document Mapping (ODM)** for non-relational databases. The Ruby interface to the HTML views is expressed via embedded Ruby files (ERB) that mix HTML and Ruby in each file.

Rails

Rails is a *web application framework*, but what is a framework? Frameworks do most of the work for an application and developers insert code where their application varies from the generic framework. This insertion of code is called *dependency injection* and we'll see numerous examples in this book. A framework is different from a library as libraries are called to assist in the development of an application, but they don't control the overall application. A simple way to tell if you're using a library or a framework is to ask,

"Did I write the main method?" If you did, you're calling libraries; if you didn't, you're using a framework. Frameworks tend to reduce the amount of code we need to write as all the "boilerplate" code already exists. A web application has a lot of interrelated parts, including the following.

1. A TCP server accepts connections from clients.
2. Code to read the headers and bodies of requests and create the headers and bodies of the responses.
3. A scheme to call the developer's code for the custom aspects of the application.
4. Error handling logic to deal appropriately with bad requests or responses.
5. Some form of templating to create dynamic HTML.
6. A method of finding and sending the CSS and JavaScript files associated with an application.
7. Creating and managing a connection to the persistent storage, typically a database management system.
8. Managing the computer resources associated with the application including the caching of resources.
9. Handling client/server state.

As developers, we're mostly interested in 3 but we need the rest to serve our application to clients. Rails and other frameworks take care of all the other aspects with very little input from us. We can choose to customize those other aspects, but Rails provides good default values so we can have a web application running with a minimum of configuration.

Rails' Conventions

Rails takes a *convention over configuration* approach to application design. There are quite a few conventions that Rails assumes you will follow and if you do, the creation of a running application can be faster than with other frameworks. Some of those other frameworks require quite a bit of creating and editing files before the application can run—for example editing many XML files to specify where the various components are in the different directories. Rails on the other hand creates a standard configuration and knows where the various components should be. An example is the creation of the `models`, `views`, and `controllers` directories in the app directory. These are three parts of the class MVC application architecture and if we follow that convention, Rails will know where to find each part and how to process it.

Here are a few of Rails' conventions that we'll see in this book.

- Model names are capitalized and singular such as Phone.
- Database tables are snake-cased (lower-cased with underscores between words) and plural such as phones.
- The data in a table are snake-cased and singular.
- Controller files are snake-cased and plural such as `phones_controller.rb`
- Controller classes are camel-cased (capitalized at the beginning of each word) such as PhonesController
- Views are in directories that are snake-cased and plural such as phones.

These do take some getting used to of course, but they tend to make the program easier to read and reduce the effort required to create, find, or fix all the moving parts of an application.

Active Record

While many of our programming languages are object-oriented (OO), the most widely used databases aren't object-oriented. This creates a mismatch that can be difficult to manage; happily, there is an approach to mapping objects to database records. Here is the high-level mapping from OO concepts to a database.

Object paradigm	Database paradigm
Class	Table
Object (instance)	Row
Variable (attribute, field)	Column
Reference	Foreign Key

An active record implementation looks at each class you want to be persisted in the database and creates a table, usually named something similar to the class's name. Each time you create a new object of a class known by the ORM, a new row is created in the associated database table with the values that the variables currently hold. The ORM monitors reads and writes to the tracked objects and updates the database appropriately.

OO languages use references for one object to gain access to another. Relational databases have a similar concept using keys. Every table in a database has what is known as a *primary key*, and this key is different for every row in a table. It is a way to uniquely identify each row. Primary keys can be several different types of data, but for this book, we'll assume they are integers. Indeed, we'll be using the default implementation for tables in relational databases which is integers starting at 1 and incrementing by 1 each time a row is added to a table. When we want to refer to data in one table to data in another, we place the primary key of the other table in a column of the table that wants to refer to it. Here are two tables that demonstrate this concept, the first is a list of people and their associated phones. The phones are stored in a different table so we use a primary key from the phones table as a foreign key for each person.

Primary key (id)	Name	Foreign key (phone_id)
1	"Laurel Elesa"	2
2	"Tessa Marie"	1

Primary key	Phone number
1	"(640) 638-1006 x318"
2	"396-410-3834 x340"

These two tables assign "Laurel Elesa" to have a telephone number of "396-410-3834 x340" and "Tessa Marie" to "(640) 638-1006 x318." In Rails, the primary key is named id while foreign keys are named *table*`_id` where `table` is the name of the referenced table and the _id refers to the primary key in that table.

While this approach isn't fully object-oriented as we're not accessing private data through methods that provide the actual functionality, it does work remarkably well to model the data relations needed in many applications. It also allows us to use appropriate tools for each part of our applications—in this case using powerful relational databases for the storage (persistence) of our application's state—while encapsulating the mapping so we don't have to be continuously cognizant of how the mapping occurs. We can program in our favorite OO language and let the ORM deal with the persistence.

Generators

Rails has many *generators* that create boilerplate, i.e. initial implementations, that are very useful. We'll mostly look at scaffolds that create all the disparate parts needed for an application, but we can create the individual parts and other necessary components using generators—we used a generator above to create migrations. To list the current generators in an application, run **rails generate**.

One to N Relationships

The easiest type of relationships are the *one-to-one* and *one-to-many*. We'll first look at the one-to-one and the options we have for the relationship between two objects.

One-to-One

An example relationship is that a person has a phone and a phone belongs to a person. We'll start out assuming phones cannot be shared between people, and every person must be assigned a phone. These are the defaults that Rails creates. Whenever we say `belongs_to`, we know it is a foreign key in one table that is the primary key in another table—this is how OO references are created in relational databases. Let's create a simple application where there are people and phones, and a person has one phone, and phones belong to a person.

Concept Leads to Code

```
rails generate scaffold Person name:string
rails generate scaffold Phone number:integer person:references

# app/models/person.rb
class Person < ApplicationRecord
  has_one :phone
end

# app/models/phone.rb
class Phone < ApplicationRecord
  belongs_to :person
end
```

The `belongs_to` is automatically created by the generator; we must add the `has_one` ourselves. Both are calls to Rails' methods or macros and allow us to reference one from the other, here a phone from a person and a person from a phone. We'll use the **`rails console`** command in this chapter to demonstrate the features of `ApplicationRecord` and the ORM. First, let's see what happens when we try to create a phone without a person (we'll use the Faker gem throughout the book to create generic data). Also note it is recommended to use the "bang" (!) form of `create` and most other Rails method calls when available, so exceptions are raised instead of always having to check the return value.

Concept Leads to Code

```
rails console
irb> Phone.create!(number: 123456789)
/Users/stevebeaty/.rbenv/versions/3.0.2/lib/ruby/gems/3.0.0/gems/
activerecord-7.0.4.3/lib/active_record/validations.rb:80:in
`raise_validation_error': Validation failed: Person must exist
(ActiveRecord::RecordInvalid)
```

This is telling us that we can't create a phone without an associated person—this may or may not be how you want to model the relationship between the data and we'll cover other options below. We can see this by running a **`sqlite3 -list db/development.sqlite3 .dump`** and looking at the SQL that creates the phones table.

Concept Leads to Code

```
CREATE TABLE IF NOT EXISTS "phones" ("id" integer PRIMARY KEY AUTOINCREMENT NOT
NULL, "number" integer, "person_id" integer NOT NULL, "created_at" datetime(6)
NOT NULL, "updated_at" datetime(6) NOT NULL, CONSTRAINT "fk_rails_06393b49b7"
FOREIGN KEY ("person_id")
  REFERENCES "people" ("id")
);
```

Note the type of the `person_id` foreign key is integer `NOT NULL` meaning there must be a reference provided. Here is the associated `db/schema.rb` file.

Concept Leads to Code

```
  ActiveRecord::Schema[7.0].define(version: 2024_03_25_144715) do
    create_table "people", force: :cascade do |t|
      t.string "name"
      t.datetime "created_at", null: false
      t.datetime "updated_at", null: false
    end

    create_table "phones", force: :cascade do |t|
      t.integer "number"
      t.integer "person_id", null: false
      t.datetime "created_at", null: false
      t.datetime "updated_at", null: false
      t.index ["person_id"], name: "index_phones_on_person_id"
    end

    add_foreign_key "phones", "people"
end
```

Let's create a person and associate two phones with them.

Concept Leads to Code

```
rails console
irb> person1=Person.create!(name: Faker::Name.name)
  TRANSACTION (0.1ms)  begin transaction
  Person Create (5.7ms)  INSERT INTO "people" ("name", "created_at",
"updated_at") VALUES (?, ?, ?)  [["name", "Yu Chen"], ["created_at", "2023-05-13
15:12:05.958571"], ["updated_at", "2023-05-13 15:12:05.958571"]]
  TRANSACTION (1.8ms)  commit transaction
=>
#<Person:0x00007fb8bc8e8e48
...
irb> Phone.create!(number: 123456789, person: person1)
  TRANSACTION (0.1ms)  begin transaction
  Phone Create (1.8ms)  INSERT INTO "phones" ("number", "person_id",
"created_at", "updated_at") VALUES (?, ?, ?, ?)  [["number", 123456789],
["person_id", 1], ["created_at", "2023-05-13 15:12:15.482633"], ["updated_at",
"2023-05-13
15:12:15.482633"]]

  TRANSACTION (1.2ms)  commit transaction
=>
#<Phone:0x00007fb8bd216998
 id: 1,
 number: 123456789,
 person_id: 1,
 created_at: Sat, 13 May 2023 15:12:15.482633000 UTC +00:00,
 updated_at: Sat, 13 May 2023 15:12:15.482633000 UTC +00:00>

irb> Phone.create!(number: 987654321, person: person1)
  TRANSACTION (0.1ms)  begin transaction
  Phone Create (0.8ms)  INSERT INTO "phones" ("number", "person_id",
"created_at", "updated_at") VALUES (?, ?, ?, ?)  [["number", 987654321],
["person_id", 4], ["created_at", "2023-05-14 08:51:36.026458"], ["updated_at",
"2023-05-14 08:51:36.026458"]]
  TRANSACTION (2.0ms)  commit transaction
=>
#<Phone:0x00007fd8cb655c38
 id: 2,
 number: 987654321,
 person_id: 4,
 created_at: Sun, 14 May 2023 08:51:36.026458000 UTC +00:00,
 updated_at: Sun, 14 May 2023 08:51:36.026458000 UTC +00:00>

irb> person1.phone.number
=> 987654321
```

We see a lot of output including the SQL statements that were executed to create the phone. From here on out, we'll elide much of the output and leave only the relevant parts to make it easier to read. Note that the person believes they have the second number associated, not both. This is due to the `has_one` relationship. Let's now create a phone, associate a phone with them, and then attempt to remove the phone.

Concept Leads to Code

```
rails console
irb> person1=Person.create!(name: Faker::Name.name)
irb> phone1=Phone.create!(number: 123456789, person: person1)
irb> person1.destroy!
  TRANSACTION (0.1ms)  begin transaction
  Person Destroy (1.2ms)  DELETE FROM "people" WHERE "people"."id" = ?  [["id",
2]]
  TRANSACTION (0.6ms)  rollback transaction
/Users/stevebeaty/.rbenv/versions/3.0.2/lib/ruby/gems/3.0.0/gems/
sqlite3-1.6.2-x86_64-darwin/lib/sqlite3/statement.rb:108:in `step':
SQLite3::ConstraintException: FOREIGN KEY constraint failed
(ActiveRecord::InvalidForeignKey)
/Users/stevebeaty/.rbenv/versions/3.0.2/lib/ruby/gems/3.0.0/gems/
sqlite3-1.6.2-x86_64-darwin/lib/sqlite3/statement.rb:108:in `step': FOREIGN KEY
constraint failed (SQLite3::ConstraintException)
```

This tells us that we've violated the constraint that the reference from a phone to a person can't be null from the `person_id integer NOT NULL` constraint from the SQL dump above.

Let's deal with how to work with both the two people attempting to share one phone, and how to allow phones to be removed from the system.

Unique

Rails allows references to be unique, here meaning that only one person can refer to a phone. When we're creating the model (or the entire MVC), we add `:uniq` to the references: **`rails generate model Phonenumber:integer person:references:uniq`**. Looking at the generated SQL we now find `CREATE UNIQUE INDEX "index_phones_on_person_id" ON "phones" ("person_id")`. We can also see this via a line in the migration file: `t.references :person, index: {:unique=>true}, null: false, foreign_key: true`. This gives us what we might want as the following demonstrates.

Concept Leads to Code

```
rails console
irb(main):001:0> person1=Person.create!(name: Faker::Name.name)
irb(main):002:0> phone1=Phone.create!(number: 123456789, person: person1)
irb(main):004:0> phone2=Phone.create!(number: 987654321, person: person1)
  TRANSACTION (0.1ms)  begin transaction
  Phone Create (0.6ms)  INSERT INTO "phones" ("number", "person_id",
"created_at", "updated_at") VALUES (?, ?, ?, ?)  [["number", 987654321],
["person_id", 1], ["created_at", "2023-05-14 09:05:20.459586"], ["updated_at",
"2023-05-14 09:05:20.459586"]]
  TRANSACTION (0.1ms)  rollback transaction
/Users/stevebeaty/.rbenv/versions/3.0.2/lib/ruby/gems/3.0.0/gems/
sqlite3-1.6.2-x86_64-darwin/lib/sqlite3/statement.rb:108:in `step':
SQLite3::ConstraintException: UNIQUE constraint failed: phones.person_id
(ActiveRecord::RecordNotUnique)
/Users/stevebeaty/.rbenv/versions/3.0.2/lib/ruby/gems/3.0.0/gems/
sqlite3-1.6.2-x86_64-darwin/lib/sqlite3/statement.rb:108:in `step': UNIQUE
constraint failed: phones.person_id (SQLite3::ConstraintException)
```

Concept Leads to Code

```
irb&glt; person1.phone.number
=glt; 987654321
```

Note however that the phone's state is such that it can't be persisted:

Concept Leads to Code

```
rails console
irb(main):008:0> person1.save!
  TRANSACTION (0.1ms)  begin transaction
  Phone Create (0.5ms)  INSERT INTO "phones" ("number", "person_id",
"created_at", "updated_at") VALUES (?, ?, ?, ?)  [["number", 987654321],
["person_id", 1], ["created_at", "2023-05-14 09:05:20.459586"], ["updated_at",
"2023-05-14 09:05:20.459586"]]
  TRANSACTION (0.1ms)  rollback transaction
/Users/stevebeaty/.rbenv/versions/3.0.2/lib/ruby/gems/3.0.0/gems/
sqlite3-1.6.2-x86_64-darwin/lib/sqlite3/statement.rb:108:in `step':
SQLite3::ConstraintException: UNIQUE constraint failed: phones.person_id
(ActiveRecord::RecordNotUnique)
/Users/stevebeaty/.rbenv/versions/3.0.2/lib/ruby/gems/3.0.0/gems/
sqlite3-1.6.2-x86_64-darwin/lib/sqlite3/statement.rb:108:in `step': UNIQUE
constraint failed: phones.person_id (SQLite3::ConstraintException)
```

We can reload the correct state using a Rails reload method, allowing us to save it to the database.

Concept Leads to Code

```
rails console
irb> person1.reload_phone
  Phone Load (0.3ms)  SELECT "phones".* FROM "phones" WHERE "phones"."person_id"
= ? LIMIT ?  [["person_id", 1], ["LIMIT", 1]]
=>
#<Phone:0x00007fd687caa2c8
 id: 1,
 number: 123456789,
 person_id: 1,
 created_at: Sun, 14 May 2023 09:04:08.737354000 UTC +00:00,
 updated_at: Sun, 14 May 2023 09:04:08.737354000 UTC +00:00>
irb(main):010:0> person1.save
=> true
```

Null

What if we want to make it possible for a phone to not have a person? We need to allow the `person_id` foreign key to be null. Note that `nil` is a value in Ruby (it is an object just like all other objects as there are methods associated with it etc.) and `NULL` is a value in SQL. `NULL` in SQL denotes there is no value, while `nil` in Ruby is a value. When we are examining objects in Ruby, `NULL` is mapped to `nil`, and there are times when we express the SQL notation using the keywords `null` or `nullify`. To allow for a `null` person for a phone we need to modify the `db/migrate/*_create_phone.rb` before we do a `rails db:migrate` to remove the `null: false` argument to the `t.references` method. Second, we need to add an `optional: true` argument to the `belongs_to` method in `app/models/phone.rb`. Finally, we want to cover the case that a person is removed and therefore need to nullify the removed person's reference in a phone; for that, we need to add `dependent: :nullify` to the `has_one` line in `app/models/person.rb`. With these in place, a phone can have a person or not.

Concept Leads to Code

```
rails console
irb> phone1=Phone.create!(number: 123456789)
irb> person1=Person.create!(name: Faker::Name.name)
irb> phone1.person=person1
irb> person1.destroy!
  TRANSACTION (0.2ms)  begin transaction
  Phone Update (1.5ms)  UPDATE "phones" SET "person_id" = ? WHERE "phones"."id"
= ?  [["person_id", nil], ["id", 1]]
  Person Destroy (0.2ms)  DELETE FROM "people" WHERE "people"."id" = ?  [["id",
1]]
  TRANSACTION (2.5ms)  commit transaction
```

We see that a phone can be created without a person and the foreign key is `nil`, that a person can be assigned later, and that when the person is destroyed the foreign key is nullified, i.e.: becomes nil. This gives us the ability to have a zero-or-more relationship.

Unique and Null

We can combine unique and null to give us a zero or one relationship.

One to Many Relationships

We've seen how the combination of `belongs_to` and `has_one` allows a relationship between a row in one table and a row in another table; there are two more ways to create those relationships. Let's first look at one-to-many relationships. In many ways, they are similar to one-to-one and indeed we were able to associate more than one person to a phone until we made that association unique. We still use the `belongs_to` to create a column for a foreign key, but we'll use `has_many` to access rows from the table that contains multiple, possibly duplicate foreign keys. Let's create a table of advisors who have many students.

Concept Leads to Code

```
rails generate scaffold Advisor name:string
rails generate scaffold Student name:string advisor:references
```

We add **`has_many :students`** to the `app/models/advisor.rb` file so we can easily refer to a list of students an advisor has. Let's create an advisor, assign three students to them, and then list those students.

Concept Leads to Code

```
rails console
irb> a1 = Advisor.create!(name: Faker::Name.name)
irb> Student.create!(name: Faker::Name.name, advisor: a1)
irb> Student.create!(name: Faker::Name.name, advisor: a1)
irb> Student.create!(name: Faker::Name.name, advisor: a1)
irb> a1.students
  Student Load (0.3ms)  SELECT "students".* FROM "students" WHERE
"students"."advisor_id" = ?  [["advisor_id", 1]]
=>
[#<Student:0x00007fedeaefc2e0
  id: 1,
  name: "Melissa Cordova",
  advisor_id: 1,
#<Student:0x00007fedeaef7c18
  id: 2,
  name: "Toni Runolfsdottir",
  advisor_id: 1,
 #<Student:0x00007fedeaef7a88
  id: 3,
  name: "Shea Love",
  advisor_id: 1,
```

We can see the `advisor_id` foreign key in each student record. If we attempt to destroy the advisor, we get the expected foreign key constraint exception and that makes sense: the loss of an advisor does not mean we should also lose the associated students. Here, we would use the techniques from the section above to allow the nullification of the foreign key in a student. There are times when one might want to destroy the dependent records, and Rails allows for that.

Let's say we have a course that has many sections. If the course needs to be removed, it might not make sense to leave the sections without the underlying course. Here are the two models.

Concept Leads to Code

```
rails generate scaffold Section number:integer course:references
rails generate scaffold Course prefix:string number:integer description:string

# app/models/course.rb
class Course < ApplicationRecord
    has_many :sections, dependent: :destroy
end
```

Let's create a course and several sections, and then destroy the course.

Concept Leads to Code

```
rails console
irb> c1 = Course.create!(prefix: "CS", number: 3710, description: "An excellent
web app class")
irb> Section.create!(number: 1, course: c1)
irb> Section.create!(number: 2, course: c1)
irb> Section.create!(number: 3, course: c1)
irb> c1.sections
  Section Load (0.3ms)  SELECT "sections".* FROM "sections" WHERE
"sections"."course_id" = ?  [["course_id", 3]]
=>
[#<Section:0x00007fa8cede8180
  id: 4,
  number: 1,
  course_id: 3,
#<Section:0x00007fa8ce6636d0
  id: 5,
  number: 2,
  course_id: 3,
#<Section:0x00007fa8ce663400
  id: 6,
  number: 3,
  course_id: 3,
  ]
irb> c1.destroy!
  TRANSACTION (0.1ms)  begin transaction
  Section Destroy (0.7ms)  DELETE FROM "sections" WHERE "sections"."id" = ?
[["id", 4]]
  Section Destroy (0.1ms)  DELETE FROM "sections" WHERE "sections"."id" = ?
[["id", 5]]
  Section Destroy (0.1ms)  DELETE FROM "sections" WHERE "sections"."id" = ?
[["id", 6]]
  Course Destroy (0.2ms)  DELETE FROM "courses" WHERE "courses"."id" = ?
[["id", 3]]
  TRANSACTION (1.5ms)  commit transaction
irb> Section.all
  Section Load (0.3ms)  SELECT "sections".* FROM "sections"
=> []
```

Here we can see when the course is destroyed, all the associated sections are too.

Many to Many Relationships

The final type of relationship is called many-to-many. These are a little more complicated than the previous relationships as we need to have an additional table, termed a junction table, to make this relationship work. A junction has two foreign keys, and usually no data itself. We refer to a junction table in the two models that need connecting.

Has Many Through

For example, students typically register for more than one section, and sections typically have more than one student, creating a many-to-many relationship. The first two tables are similar to what they have been so far. Here is an example students table.

Primary key	Name
5	"Dee Harper, Ph.D."
6	"Johnnie Wehner"
7	"Toby S. Cat, Esq."
8	"Harmony Ortiz, DO"

And an example sections table.

Primary key	Name
4	"CS3700"
5	"CS3710"
6	"CS3755"

The junction table has foreign keys from each of the two tables above and this allows us to assign many students to a course and courses to a student.

section_id	student_id
4	5
5	5
4	6

Generating the junction table is straightforward as we know how to create the references: **`rails generate scaffold Registration section:references student:references`** and the other two tables are easy from the data they contain **`rails generate scaffold Section name:string`** and **`rails generate scaffold Student name:string`**.

We do have to change the model files for both as we did before for `has_one` or `has_many`, though now we must describe how to reference the other data using the junction table.

Concept Leads to Code

```
# app/models/section.rb
class Section < ApplicationRecord
      has_many :registrations
      has_many :students, through: :registrations
end

# app/models/student.rb
class Student < ApplicationRecord
      has_many :registrations
      has_many :sections, through: :registrations
end
```

Assuming the students and sections table contains the data in the tables above, we can add sections to a student and vice versa.

Concept Leads to Code

```
rails console
irb> Student.find(5).sections.push(Section.find(4))
irb> Student.find(5).sections.push(Section.find(5))
irb> Section.find(4).students.push(Student.find(6))
irb> Student.find(5).sections
[#<Section:0x00007fe5a03509e8 id: 4, name: "CS3700">,
 #<Section:0x00007fe5a0350880 id: 5, name: "CS3710">]
irb> Section.find(4).students
[#<Student:0x00007fe5a73b6bd8 id: 5, name: "Alden Blick">,
 #<Student:0x00007fe5a73b6ae8 id: 6, name: "Johnnie Wehner">]
```

Has and Belongs to Many

Another approach to many-to-many relations is Rails' *has_and_belongs_to_many (HABTM)* relationship. It is very similar to the *has_many_through* relationship but is slightly terser. A junction table is still required of course, and we still must create it explicitly. The name of the junction table follows a very specific convention so that Rails can find it and reference the two associated tables. The name of the junction table is not specified in either of the model files but is implied by the alphabetic (lexigraphic) order of the table names. The junction table name to connect students and sections must be named *SectionsStudents* for Rails to recognize it as a junction table. Creating the three tables is relatively straightforward.

Concept Leads to Code

```
rails g scaffold Section name:string
rails g scaffold Student name:string
rails g scaffold SectionsStudents section:references student:references --force-
plural
```

The -force-plural is necessary to override Rails' general conventions. The model files are similar to what we've seen before.

Concept Leads to Code

```
# app/models/section.rb
class Section < ApplicationRecord
    has_and_belongs_to_many :students
end

# app/models/student.rb
class Student < ApplicationRecord
    has_and_belongs_to_many :sections
end
```

Now, we can reference students from sections and sections from students.

Concept Leads to Code

```
rails console
irb> Student.create!(name: Faker::Name.name)
irb> Student.create!(name: Faker::Name.name)
irb> Student.create!(name: Faker::Name.name)
irb> Section.create!(name: "CS3700")
irb> Section.create!(name: "CS3710")
irb> Section.create!(name: "CS3755")
irb> Student.find(1).sections.push(Sections.find(1))
irb> Student.find(1).sections.push(Sections.find(2))
irb> Student.find(1).sections
[#<Section:0x00007fe30d00de88 id: 1, name: "CS3700">,
 #<Section:0x00007fe30d00dd98 id: 2, name: "CS3710">]
irb> Section.find(1).students
[#<Student:0x00007fe30b50ead8 id: 1, name: "Ms. Jermaine Durgan">]
```

Mixing Relationships

Of course, many data are interrelated to many other data, in various forms. Consider a section of a course: it has a course (one-to-one), a semester (one-to-one), possibly cross-listings (one-to-many) and many students (many-to-many). This means we must carefully consider how our application's data are related to each other and choose models that reflect those relationships. When we do, our application's logic is greatly simplified, when we don't, we find ourselves creating a morass of special-case code throughout our applications.

Testing Models

This will be our first foray into testing our application. A widely used approach to developing software is called **Test-Driven Development (TDD)**. The general outline of TDD is as follows.

1. Write a test for the change you want to make. This could be new code or a modification to existing code. You should be able to write the test before the code as you know what the code should do. Indeed, if you can't write the test, how can you be sure the result of your code is correct?
2. Run all the relevant tests using a test framework. All should pass except the one (or more) tests you just wrote. If the new test(s) pass, something is wrong, and you'll need to figure out what.
3. Write just enough code to make the test pass. We are all tempted to write more than we need thinking that we'll need the code someday. The acronym *Ya Ain't Gonna Need It (YAGNI)* addresses this temptation. Essentially it states that don't write any code that you don't need right now. We're bad at predicting what we'll need. We'll have to maintain the YAGNI code for perpetuity even if it's never used. We also probably added to the API of the class and the YAGNI code almost certainly does something, even if it's something no one needs, and it increases the exploit surface of our application.
4. Run the tests and make sure they pass.
5. Refactor. We learn things about the problem, our programming language, and our solution as we test and create code. We must improve the code when we find redundancies, inefficient code, and errors. This process is called refactoring. If the fix is quick, doing this during the TDD cycle is a good idea. If the fix will take a significant amount of time, it probably needs to be a separate task in the project management system so that it is tracked.

TDD is popular for many reasons. First, it puts you in a different frame of mind. When we write tests, we think "How can I break this? Under what circumstances should/shouldn't this work?" in addition to the usual "How can I make this work?" code tends to be more resilient when we consider what doesn't work in addition to what does. TDD also creates a lot of regression tests that allow for effective *Continuous Integration/ Continuous Deployment (CI/CD)* pipelines. CI/CD are those development environments that keep repositories and/or branches in a ready-to-ship state. CI/CD pipelines often monitor for repository check-ins and then run the test suite on the new code. Depending on the sophistication of the tests, the new code may either be accepted or rejected into the repository or be immediately deployed if all tests pass.

It is also very important that we document the circumstances a method should and should not work and unit tests are used for this purpose too. The tests document when we expect a method to run or throw an exception. Consider a method with two numbers as parameters. Unit tests should document what should happen with positive, negative, zero, Not A Number (in Ruby: `Float::NAN`), and the two infinities (`Float::INFINITY` and `-Float::INFINITY`) are passed to each argument. A very general rule of thumb is that there should be as many lines of test code as there are for production code. Half your lines, but maybe not half your time, will be used for testing. Another major upside to TDD and having a large regression test suite is it removes a certain amount of fear when we create new code or refactor. If we know our changes don't break code either locally or globally, we can more easily improve the code base.

Rails automatically creates a directory hierarchy for testing and creates some initial tests for several parts of an application. Here are the top-level directories; we'll be looking at many of them throughout this book.

Concept Leads to Code

```
application_system_test_case.rb
channels/
controllers/
fixtures/
helpers/
integration/
mailers/
models/
system/
test_helper.rb
```

Rails names the directories to reflect their use. In this chapter, we'll be looking at creating model tests so we'll be working on files in the models directory.

First, you must make sure your YAML fixture files in test/fixtures have information that is correct for any database constraints you placed on any of the fields, such as using uniq when you created a model, migration, or scaffold. Anytime **`rails test`** is run, the fixtures are loaded into a test database, and any errors there will interfere with the testing of your models. For example, the following YAML file makes the identifier, phone, email, and URL strings unique.

Concept Leads to Code

```
# test/fixtures/people.yml
one:
  identifier: 1
  first_name: MyString
  last_name: MyString
  phone: MyString1
  email: MyString1
  url: MyString1

two:
  identifier: 2
  first_name: MyString
  last_name: MyString
  phone: MyString2
  email: MyString2
  url: MyString2
```

Many-to-many tests require a little more care. We need to communicate to Rails what classes are used for the junction table. For the HABTM relationship, we must add a few things to the `test_helper.rb` file. We must set the fixture class Rails will use, and importantly: we might have to change the order in which fixtures are run. By default, it's alphabetical, but if we have junction tables, that probably won't work. We need to change the `fixtures :all` statement to list the proper order of loading fixtures.

Concept Leads to Code

```
# test/test_helper.rb
[…]
  set_fixture_class books_libraries: BooksLibraries
[…]
  fixtures :books, :libraries, :books_libraries
```

If we use the `has_many through` approach, we also need to change the model file so that the tests will run.

Concept Leads to Code

```
class Book < ApplicationRecord
  has_many :books_libraries, class_name: 'BooksLibraries'
  has_many :libraries, through: :books_libraries
end
```

Model Validation

We must validate all data placed into databases. Once a database contains invalid data, the task of cleaning up can become monumental. It is also the case that allowing bad data can lead to security issues. The new method doesn't run model **validations**, but `create`, `create!`, `save`, `save!`, `update`, `update!` all do. Rails provides a number of different ways to validate data, including the following.

1. acceptance
    a. Validates that a check box was checked.
2. validates_associated
    a. Checks to make sure a has_one or has_many association holds.
3. confirmation
    a. Checks to make sure that two associated fields are identical more here.
4. comparison
    a. Confirms that a value is between two values. Any value that includes Comparable works. Here is the list of comparisons.
        i. :greater_than
        ii. :greater_than_or_equal_to

            iii. :equal_to
            iv. :less_than
            v. :less_than_or_equal_to
            vi. :other_than
5. exclusion
    a. Confirms that a value is not in an enumerable.
6. format
    a. Validates that a value matches a regular expression.
7. inclusion
    a. Confirms that a value is in an enumerable.
8. length
    a. Validates that the length of a value has a minimum or maximum length, or within a range.
9. numericality
    a. Confirms the value is a number. There are a number of additional validations that can be checked.
        i. :greater_than
        ii. :greater_than_or_equal_to
        iii. :equal_to
        iv. :less_than
        v. :less_than_or_equal_to
        vi. :other_than
        vii. :in
        viii. :odd
        ix. :even
10. presence
    a. Validates that a value is present. You probably shouldn't use this as the mere presence of a value typically isn't enough to assure its validity.
11. absence
    a. The opposite of presence.
12. uniqueness
    a. Checks to see if there are any other identical values. This is different than the 'uniq' database qualifier but can be used to achieve the same effect.
13. validates_with
    a. Specifies a method that performs the checks necessary to validate a particular field. This can be used when the checks involve multiple fields and conditions that can't be expressed with the other validations.

Here is a model that includes a number of different validations. Note the `before_validation` method call: it is another example of dependency injection where we provide the framework with a method to call before/after an event. Of course, all the validation method calls are also dependency injections—they happen before an object is persisted. All these validations are a bit naive, and you should customize all your validations to reflect how data must look in your database. Also, note that Ruby comes with regular expressions for email addresses and URLs. You can express valid values with ranges, minimum/maximum, and possibly greater_than/less_than etc.

Concept Leads to Code

```
# app/models/person.rb
class Person < ApplicationRecord
  before_validation :sanitize_phone_number
  validates :identifier, numericality: {in: 900_000_000..999_999_999}
  validates_format_of :url, with: URI::regexp
  validates_format_of :email, with: URI::MailTo::EMAIL_REGEXP
  validates :first_name, length: { in: 2..25 }
  validates :phone, format: {with: /\A[0-9]{10}\z/}

  private
    def sanitize_phone_number
      self.phone = self.phone.gsub(/[^0-9]/, '') if self.phone
    end
end
```

Model Testing Example

When we're testing any part of our application, the general approach is as follows.

1. Given. What are our assumptions about the state of the application? What do the data look like? Are they valid? What will the code do to the data?
2. When. When the state changes, is the new state valid or not? What are the changes to the data and what does the code do to the state?
3. Then. What is the new state of the application? That is, what are all the values the application holds? Of course, we hopefully don't change many values while testing a specific portion of the code—this is part of the reason we follow object-oriented coding practices assiduously. If the user (or test) passes invalid data, what does the application do? It should of course not accept the data while not crashing.

To test our model validations, we need to consider both the cases that should pass and those that shouldn't. It is recommended that you always use the '!' case for creating, updating, etc. objects so that errors are quickly observed and fixed. Here is a file that tests for both the successful and unsuccessful creation of objects given the above validations. The unsuccessful tests make sure an assertion is raised and check that the error message is related to the failing validation. These tests are not complete; they demonstrate one approach to testing that data that are persisted are in some way correct.

The "given" here is a currently clean database, the "when" is when we attempt to create a new person, and the "then" is whether the person is created, or an exception is raised. We also check the message if an exception is raised to make sure the error message is correct.

You should of course write the tests before writing the validations as part of your TDD practice. If you don't know how to test your code, you probably don't know enough to write it.

Concept Leads to Code

```
# test/models/person_test.rb
require "test_helper"

class PersonTest < ActiveSupport::TestCase
  test 'good person' do
    person = Person.create!(first_name: "AA", last_name: "AA",
    identifier: 900_000_000, url: "https://example.com", email: "a@b.c",
    phone: "1234567890")
  end

  test 'first name too short' do
    exception = assert_raise(ActiveRecord::RecordInvalid) {
      person = Person.create!(first_name: "A", last_name: "AA",
      identifier: 900_000_000, url: "https://example.com", email: "a@b.c",
      phone: "1234567890")
    }
    assert_equal(exception.message, "Validation failed: First name is too short
(minimum is 2 characters)")
  end

  test 'first name too long' do
    exception = assert_raise(ActiveRecord::RecordInvalid) {
      person = Person.create!(first_name: "AAAAAAAAAAAAAAAAAAAAAAAAAA",
      last_name: "AA", identifier: 900_000_000, url: "https://example.com",
      email: "a@b.c", phone: "1234567890")
    }
    assert_equal(exception.message, "Validation failed: First name is too long
(maximum is 25 characters)")
  end

  test 'identifier too small' do
    exception = assert_raise(ActiveRecord::RecordInvalid) {
      person = Person.create!(first_name: "AA", last_name: "AA",
      identifier: 9, url: "https://example.com", email: "a@b.c",
      phone: "1234567890")
    }
    assert_equal(exception.message, "Validation failed: Identifier must be in
900000000..999999999")
  end

  test 'identifier too big' do
    exception = assert_raise(ActiveRecord::RecordInvalid) {
      person = Person.create!(first_name: "AA", last_name: "AA",
      identifier: 1_000_000_000, url: "https://example.com", email: "a@b.c",
      phone: "1234567890")
    }
    assert_equal(exception.message, "Validation failed: Identifier must be in
900000000..999999999")
  end

  test 'bad url' do
    exception = assert_raise(ActiveRecord::RecordInvalid) {
```

```
      person = Person.create!(first_name: "AA", last_name: "AA",
      identifier: 900_000_000, url: "badurl", email: "a@b.c",
      phone: "1234567890")
    }
    assert_equal(exception.message, "Validation failed: Url is invalid")
  end

  test 'bad email' do
    exception = assert_raise(ActiveRecord::RecordInvalid) {
      person = Person.create!(first_name: "AA", last_name: "AA",
      identifier: 900_000_000, url: "https://example.com", email: "a",
      phone: "1234567890")
    }
    assert_equal(exception.message, "Validation failed: Email is invalid")
  end

  test 'phone too short' do
    exception = assert_raise(ActiveRecord::RecordInvalid) {
      person = Person.create!(first_name: "AA", last_name: "AA",
      identifier: 900_000_000, url: "https://example.com", email: "a@b.c",
      phone: "12345678")
    }
    assert_equal(exception.message, "Validation failed: Phone is invalid")
  end

  test 'phone too long' do
    exception = assert_raise(ActiveRecord::RecordInvalid) {
      person = Person.create!(first_name: "AA", last_name: "AA",
      identifier: 900_000_000, url: "https://example.com", email: "a@b.c",
      phone: "12345678901")
    }
    assert_equal(exception.message, "Validation failed: Phone is invalid")
  end

  test 'good phone with dashes' do
    person = Person.create!(first_name: "AA", last_name: "AA",
    identifier: 900_000_000, url: "https://example.com", email: "a@b.c",
    phone: "123-456-7890")
  end

  test 'good phone with spaces' do
    person = Person.create!(first_name: "AA", last_name: "AA",
    identifier: 900_000_000, url: "https://example.com", email: "a@b.c",
    phone: "123 456 7890")
  end

  test 'good phone with parens, spaces, and dashes' do
    person = Person.create!(first_name: "AA", last_name: "AA",
    identifier: 900_000_000, url: "https://example.com", email: "a@b.c",
    phone: "(123) 456-7890")
  end
end
```

Non-Relational Databases

Non-relational databases (often called NoSQL databases, erroneously) have gained a lot of attention recently, even though they've been around for a long time. Much of their popularity is due to their efficiency and speed for typical operations. They are not modeled in terms of tables and relationships between tables. They tend not to have a schema in the traditional sense, but that does not mean we don't have to create an efficient and effective model for them; non-relational databases can be every bit as inefficient as any other if we don't create them properly.

Non-relational databases reflect the changing nature of web applications. For example, some give up consistency (the idea that reads reflect the most recent write) for speed. For a typical social media application, this isn't a problem as everyone will see a write eventually (here, eventually typically means a second or less). Relational databases continue to be used when this type of consistency matters: bank accounts, reservation systems, etc. (i.e.: whenever there is a shared resource that costs the end user actual money). Given that we don't need immediate consistency, not only might our general transactions be faster, but our applications might also be easier to scale horizontally. That is, adding virtual machines, and computer resources (cores, memory, disk space, etc.) will increase the responsiveness of our application. This is a boon in the cloud and other environments where we can scale (and pay) for the increased needs only when necessary. The guarantees relational databases make about transactions can make them more difficult to scale across many machines, memory, and disks.

Normalization

We must also address the **normalization** of databases. Normalization informally means that there is no duplication of data (*first normal form* (1NF)), that columns don't contain composite values (2NF), that there are no transitive dependencies between columns in a table (3NF), and so on. Rails' ORM helps us with some of these by, e.g.: providing a primary key for each table. We can, if we know the data well, override this. Non-relational databases allow us to choose to violate normalization and indeed this may occur often in their creation and use. For example, let's say there is an avatar image associated with each account. A relational database would create a table of avatars and when a user's avatar is changed, it would only need to update the image in one place for it to be reflected everywhere. The update is efficient, but every time a user's posts are displayed a foreign key must be followed. A non-relational database might choose to embed the avatar image in each record of the user's posts. Changing the avatar would require traversing all the user's documents and updating each with the new avatar image. A question becomes: how often are avatar images changed versus how often are posts displayed? Here is the tradeoff: relational databases make the updating fast, but the display of a post is probably slower, with non-relational databases having the opposite efficiency. Non-relational databases will sometimes choose to not be normalized to gain efficiency in access.

MongoDB

MongoDB (https://www.mongodb.com) is a widely used non-relational database, based on a document model. There are other non-relational database models such as key/value pairs, trees, etc. MongoDB does provide for consistency across multi-document writes when the appropriate methods are called. MongoDB is a play on the word huMONGOus as it is designed with large datasets in mind. MongoDB uses *BSON* (*Binary JavaScript Object Notation*) that extends the types available in JSON and is a format that allows for fast searching as it includes the current document size in every header so finding the next document is a matter of reading that many bytes. As with all data representations, there are tradeoffs associated with BSON; the faster searching comes at a price of possibly slower writes. This tradeoff is appropriate for certain types of web applications, and less so for others. We need to consider the most typical operations we need to perform with our data and choose the appropriate database technology.

Installing

A prerequisite to using MongoDB in an ODM is having a MongoDB server running on your local machine. This is a little different than we've seen before with SQLite3 in that MongoDB will be an independent process instead of part of the Rails server. This is also the case when we use many other relational databases such as PostgreSQL, MariaDB, Oracle, etc., of course. The Rails server will interact with MongoDB via port number 27017 on the local machine. Here is where you can download the server: https://www.mongodb.com/try/download/community. In addition to the server, you probably want to download mongosh (the Mongo shell) and MongoDB Compass (a MongoDB GUI) from https://www.mongodb.com/try/download/tools.

For MacOS, brew has formulae for mongo-server, mongo-database-tools, and mongosh. To start the server, type **`brew services start mongodb-community`** and to stop type **`brew services stop mongodb-community`**.

For the MongoDB shell, running **`mongosh`** is equivalent to `mongosh "mongodb://localhost:27017"`. This is the default machine name and port number for MongoDB.

Relationships

MongoDB is capable of the usual one-to-one, one-to-many, and many-to-many relationships we saw above in ORMs. Let's start with a simple one-to-one relationship. The `-skip-active-record` argument does exactly that: skips adding the gem needed for an ORM; we need to add mongoid so we can use it as an ODM.

Concept Leads to Code

```
rails new one2one --minimal --skip-active-record
cd one2one
bundle add faker
bundle add mongoid
rails generate mongoid:config # creates config/mongoid.yml
rails generate scaffold Person name:string
rails generate scaffold Phone number:integer person:references
```

We must put a `has_one :phone` in `app/models/person.rb` as `has_one` is not a database relationship but a macro for exposing additional methods to a person via Rails' ODM. For many-to-many relationships, MongoDB doesn't need a junction table as it can store arrays of references directly in a document. MongoDB also creates a document identifier based on the time since the epoch, a random number, and a randomly incremented counter so we can reference a document directly from another document.

Let's also create a `db/seeds.rb` to initialize some data. If we don't use Active Record, no `db` directory is created and of course there is no `db/schema.rb` nor `db/migrate/*` files, so we must first create the `db` directory and the the `seeds.rb` file in that.

Concept Leads to Code

```
# db/seeds.rb
require "faker"

Phone.destroy_all
Person.destroy_all

20.times do
  person=Person.create!(name: Faker::Name.name)
  number = Phone.create!(number: rand(100000000..999999999), person: person)
end
```

Even though Active Record isn't being used, Rails still knows how to perform the **`rails db:seed`** command. To see the resulting databases, you can use the mongoexport tool via **`mongoexport —db one2one_development -collection people`** and **`mongoexport —db one2one_development -collection phones`**.

You can also use rails console and do **`Phone.all.to_a`** and **`Person.all.to_a`**. Note, that this is slightly different than when using Active Record; here the `.all` returns a collection but doesn't query it for performance reasons; the `.to_a` forces the query.

Another way to see the results of the seeding, and of course, further Rails' interactions with the database is via `mongosh`. We can show the databases, choose one, show the collections, and show the contents of a particular collection.

Concept Leads to Code

```
mongosh
one2one_development> show databases
admin                                               40.00 KiB
config                                              36.00 KiB
local                                               80.00 KiB
one2one_development                                144.00 KiB
one2one_test                                        48.00 KiB
one2one_development> use one2one_development
one2one_development> show collections
people
phones
one2one_development> db.phones.find()
[...]
```

A final way is to use the MongoDB Compass GUI to connect to the MongoDB server and find the appropriate databases and collections that way. While all these methods show essentially the same data, it is important to know what exactly is in a database/collection and having multiple approaches will help you during development.

Embedding

While it is useful to reference other documents in a relational style, MongoDB's power typically comes from *embedding* one model within another. This is how relationships are typically formed and where much of the performance is gained. If a phone is embedded in a person for example, when we fetch a person from the database, we also retrieve their phone number in a single read. If we instead reference a phone from a person, we don't retrieve their phone on a read of their record, the database must perform a second read to retrieve it. In an OO language, this is similar to *chasing references* in a linked data structure. This is where database design becomes important. A question is "How often do we want a person's phone number when we retrieve their data?" If it is 100% of the time, then embedding makes the most sense. If the answer is rarely, then referencing might be more appropriate to keep the size of the read smaller. If we only embed a single model in another it might make sense to put the data in the outer document directly. Embedding typically makes more sense when we have multiple objects (documents) embedded in one another.

Embeds Many

One example of an application that makes good use of embedding is a social media platform that allows for articles to be written and comments made on those articles. Here, we want to display the comments along with an article so embedding comments within an article both makes sense and retrieving all the comments when retrieving an article can increase the responsiveness of the application. This will probably be faster than having a one-to-many relationship where the database would have to find all the comments that match an article. We also designed this application so there are no standalone comments; that is, all CRUD operations on comments will be called from an article page. Nesting the comment routes inside of the article routes maps this concept very well.

Concept Leads to Code

```
Rails.application.routes.draw do
  resources :articles do
    resources :comments, only: [:new, :create]
  end
end
```

Here are two routes from the above routes file that show comments are created through an articles URL but call two methods in the comments controller and pass in the current article identifier.

Concept Leads to Code

```
              Prefix Verb   URI Pattern                  Controller#Action
   article_comments POST   /articles/:article_id/comments(.:format)
comments#create
new_article_comment GET    /articles/:article_id/comments/new(.:format)
comments#new
```

As this namespaces comments under articles, we need to update the partial `app/views/comments/_form.html.erb` to start with `<%= form_with model: [:article, comment] do |form| %>`. We also want to remove the link "Back to comments" as there is no reason to have a list of comments, something that would require iterating on all the articles and gathering all the comments.

We can create both the articles and comments scaffolding as usual using strings for the values, but we need to add the embedding manually, so the models look like the following.

Concept Leads to Code

```
class Article
  include Mongoid::Document
  include Mongoid::Timestamps
  field :text, type: String
  embeds_many :comments
end

class Comment
  include Mongoid::Document
  include Mongoid::Timestamps
  field :text, type: String
  embedded_in :article
end
```

We of course need to modify the comments controller to use this information. Along with creating a new comment, we need to embed it in the associated article. We find the article using `article_id` parameter and then append the new comment. We also need to change the redirect after the save so that the article is displayed that now contains the comment. The other CRUD operations will need to be updated similarly.

Concept Leads to Code

```
def create
  @comment = Comment.new(comment_params)
  article = Article.find(params[:article_id])
  article.comments << @comment

  if @comment.save
    redirect_to article, notice: "Comment was successfully created."
  else
    render :new, status: :unprocessable_entity
  end
end
```

When we display an article, we want to display the associated comments and have the ability to create more comments. Updating the `app/views/articles/_article.html.erb` partial to the following does both of these.

Concept Leads to Code

```
<div id="Text:</strong>
    <%= article.text %>
  </p>
  <p>
    <strong>Comments:</strong>
    <%= render article.comments %>
  </p>
  <%= link_to "New comment", new_article_comment_path(article.id) %>
</div>
```

Non-Relational Summary

Non-relational databases come with many benefits and few drawbacks. They tend to reflect the evolving nature of web applications in some of the following ways.

- Write once and read many.
- The hierarchy of data, in the example above comments don't exist without being part of an article.
- The possible lessening of strict requirements on data such as the necessity of immediate consistency in the database.

Summary

This has been a long chapter with a lot of information. This is appropriate as applications are data manipulation engines. We, at least at some level, don't care how the data are changed, just that they are. That is the essence of computing: changing data from one form to another. If data aren't changed, why run a program? We have covered how Rails manipulates data in both relational and non-relational databases. We have covered how data are validated and how our models are tested. If we get the data portion of our applications correct, the rest of the implementation is more straightforward. If we don't, we'll forever be working around the representation.

Exercises

Directions: Use what you learned in this chapter to complete the following tasks and exercises.

1. Create the models necessary for a simple course management system with the following relationships.
   a. A course has a prefix, a number, a description, and many sections.
   b. A semester has a year, Spring/Summer/Fall, and many sections.
   c. An instructor has a name and many sections.
   d. A section belongs to a course, a semester, students, and an instructor.
   e. A student has a name and many sections.
2. Write a `db/seeds.rb` file for the above.
3. Make sure all the `tests/fixture/*.yml` files are appropriate for the above so that `rails test` runs with no errors.
4. Write validations for the above and make sure all the tests run.
5. Create an ODM where a person has many (embeds many) email addresses.

CHAPTER 4

Views

"My father says that there is only one perfect view, that of the sky over our heads."

E. M. Forster, A Room with a View.

Introduction

The second aspect of the MVC model is the view. It's probably the most familiar (with many knowing the rudiments of HTML, CSS, and JavaScript), but too often the least emphasized. *User interface/user experience (UI/UX)* makes a large difference in people's acceptance of a web application. We need to create applications that are both compelling and easy to use. Rails includes a module named Action View that helps with many aspects of creating the views that users interact with.

Learning Outcomes

By the end of this chapter, you'll be able to do the following.

1. Create views of your application data that users find easy to use.
2. Make your applications localized for wider use.
3. Make your applications accessible.
4. Keep your application DRY using metaprogramming, partials, and **helper functions**.
5. Assure that your application is multi-display friendly, allowing users with cell phones or large monitors to find your application equally compelling.
6. Create applications that react to new data.
7. Make your web applications similar to native applications.
8. Use Ajax and alternative JavaScript frontends to create an application.

Key Terms

The following important **terms** will be introduced in this chapter.

- **Accessibility**
- **Templating and embedding**
- **Metaprogramming**
- **Helper functions**
- **Partials**

- **Responsive**
- **On-Demand or Just in Time (JIT)**
- **Continuous Integration/Continuous Deployment (CI/CD)**
- **JSON API**

Accessibility

Whenever we create applications, we need to make them **accessible** to all. This not only increases the audience for our applications, but it is also the only ethical approach to creating applications. We must not deny access to anyone. The major guidelines for the accessibility of web applications are found in the *Web Content Accessibility Guidelines (WCAG)* 2.0 (https://www.w3.org/TR/WCAG20/). These guidelines are the basis of the U.S. government's 508 standards (https://www.access-board.gov/ict/). There are numerous tools you can use to ensure your web application is accessible; one published by the W3C can be found at https://www.w3.org/WAI/eval/report-tool/. It is crucial that the applications we create do not contribute to the digital divide; everyone must be able to participate in society. Rails helps with accessibility but is not a complete solution for creating an accessible web application.

Embedded Ruby (ERB)

For HTML, the default way to render results is via an Embedded Ruby (ERB) file. These are template files processed using Ruby, having values passed from their associated controllers. Rails uses the convention of calling the template named after the method in a controller, specified in the `config/routes.rb` file, for rendering (display) purposes. This makes the templates easy to find as they exist in the `app/views/name` directory. There are three main delimiters in ERB.

1. `<% ... %>`

Run the Ruby code between the delimiters, but don't place the output in the resulting HTML. Remember that Ruby has expressions where other languages have statements so that many expressions create a result that we might not need to show in the HTML. For example, the loop `10.times` {} returns 10 even though the loop is empty, and we probably don't want to display the 10 in the HTML.

1. `<%= ... %>`

Run the Ruby code between the delimiters and put the result in the HTML.

1. `<%# ... %>`

A comment that isn't placed in the resulting HTML and is mostly useful for commenting out Ruby code during development.

Other frameworks use other delimiters, with {{ ... }} being a popular alternative. Regardless, each framework has HTML (and often JSON) templates to allow the easy separation of HTML, CSS, JavaScript, and the backend language.

Here is a simple template from a todo application in the file `app/views/items/index.html.erb`.

Concept Leads to Code

```
<p style="color: green"><%= notice %></p>

<h1>Items</h1>

<div id="items">
  <% @items.each do |item| %>
    <%= render item %>
    <p>
      <%= link_to "Show this item", item %>
    </p>
  <% end %>
</div>

<%= link_to "New item", new_item_path %>
```

This shows both major delimiters, one that doesn't create output for the `@items.each`, and one that does create output for all other uses of Ruby. This template also shows several other aspects of ERBs: view helpers and partials.

View Helpers

We see two `link_to` helpers in the ERB code above, one a link to item and another to `new_item_path`. These two values are created by the Rails routing mechanisms which will be covered in more depth in the chapter on controllers. For the time being, we can look at the output of **`rails routes`**; one line shows `item GET /items/:id(.:format) items#show` and another `new_item GET /items/new(.:format) items#new`. The first column is the helper, the second the HTTP verb, the third the URL that is the request match, and the final column is the controller and method name associated with the request. The `link_to` with `item` will match the first route we see here and send the associated request. Note that the `link_to` will vary for each item—the URL will have the form `/items/#` to display the associated item directly. A nice aspect of not hard-coding the request in the HTML is when routes change, this ERB file doesn't have to. The second `link_to` creates a link to the page for creating a completely new item and uses the `_path` suffix that generates a relative path; there is also the `_url` to reference the absolute path.

There are `button_to` and `url_to` helpers similar to the `link_to` helper.

Partials

Partials are ERB templates, but not for an entire page (hence "partial"). They are used to keep your redundant code out of your application, i.e.: to keep it DRY. *DRY* means *Don't Repeat Yourself*—have only one copy of any code, be it HTML, JavaScript, CSS, Ruby, etc. When we have more than one copy, we must remember where all the copies are, a difficult task at best. What we instead do is refer to code that we already have from where it is needed. In this way, one fix fixes all instances, and we don't have to hunt down all the instances to change or fix an aspect of our application. The render method takes the name of a partial template file to call, the convention is to place an underscore at the beginning of the file name to specify it's a partial. So, for the `render item` above, Rails renders the `app/views/items/_item.html.erb` file. A partial reduces redundancy for this application as both `index.html.erb` and `show.html.erb` show one or more items.

Partials can also be used to easily render collections for has_many relationships. For example, if an advisor has many students, you can put a `render @advisor.students` in the `app/views/advisor/show.html.erb` file.

Concept Leads to Code

```
<div id="<%= dom_id advisor %>">
  <p>
    <strong>Name:</strong>
    <%= advisor.name %>
  </p>

  <%# This works %>
  <p>
    <strong>Students:</strong>
    <% advisor.students.each do |student| %>
      <%= render student %>
    <% end %>
  </p>

  <%# So does this %>
  <p>
    <strong>Students:</strong>
    <%= render advisor.students %>
  </p>
</div>
```

You'll have to be careful using render in `has_many through` and `has_and_belongs_to_many` views as if both sides use the collection render, an infinite loop will occur. One side of the view needs to use a loop.

Internationalization (I18N) and Localization (L10N)

All applications should be available to as wide an audience as possible, regardless of their native country or language. This dramatically expands our audience and makes our content much more approachable.

Internationalization (called I18N as it is spelled with and an I, 18 other letters, then an N) is the process of making our applications multi-lingual. We don't use explicit strings in our application, instead create places where strings can automatically be substituted on demand. As of this writing, Rails ships with 121 localization files in the I18N gem. These are YAML files that contain information such as the following.

- Day and month names, and the order of year/month/day.
- The time.
- Some error messages.
- The words for select/create/submit/update.
- Currency display.
- The words for thousand/million/billion etc.
- Et cetera.

There are two basic methods Rails uses for *localization* (called L10N for the same reason as above): `translate` and `localize` (these have the aliases t and l for shorthand use).

We can also create translation files. A very simple and naive German translation into YAML of our todo items could look like the following.

Concept Leads to Code

```
# config/locales/de.yml
de:
  item: "Machen"
  items: "Machen"
  what: "Was"
  when: "Wann"
```

These values can then be used in the various views as part of ERB code.

Concept Leads to Code

```
# app/views/items/index.html.erb
<h1><%= t :items %></h1>

# app/views/items/_item.html.erb
<div id="<%= dom_id item %>">
  <p>
    <strong><%= t :what %></strong>
    <%= item.what %>
  </p>

  <p>
    <strong><%= t :when %></strong>
    <%= item.when %>
  </p>
</div>

# app/views/items/edit.html.erb
<h1>Editing item</h1>

<%= t :item %>
<%= render "form", item: @item %>
```

There are many ways to set the language used for your application, including the following.

- Domain name.
- URL parameters.
- User preferences.
- Request headers.

We can also set it globally as follows.

Concept Leads to Code

```
# config/application.rb
module I18N
  class Application < Rails::Application

    # [...]

    config.i18n.default_locale = :de

    # [...]

  end
end
```

Rich Text

Rails comes with a rich text editor called Trix but note this isn't a Rich Text Format (RTF) editor, but an HTML editor that integrates easily with the framework. Trix is part of the Action Text module, but you'll need to install it via the command line. Trix allows attachments such as images, but you'll also need to install a graphics library on your server for this work; libvips (https://www.libvips.org/) and ImageMagick (https://www.imagemagick.org/) are both supported. Active Storage is also needed for attachments, with the default storage going to the `storage` directory in the root directory of the application. Active Storage has many other places it can store attachments including many of the cloud storage providers. Happily, the defaults just work; here's a short script to create a message application that uses rich text.

Concept Leads to Code

```
rails new trix
cd trix
bin/rails action_text:install
rails generate scaffold Message content:rich_text
bin/rails db:migrate
```

Style

In Rails, links are typically used for GETs, and buttons for POSTs. This reflects REST but leads to some visual inconsistencies in bare Rails applications. For example, Rails uses GETs (links) for showing and editing, but POSTs (buttons) for updating and destroying items. This is consistent with RESTfulness but can look weird for end users used to everything being a button. There are several approaches to dealing with this; creating forms that use GETs and using CSS are two.

Creating Forms for Links

An approach to creating buttons instead of links is to create a short form but specify the method as being GET instead of the default POST. A simple example can be shown using the `index.html.erb` file in any scaffolded view. Several things to note in the following code.

1. We use the `form_with` helper from Rails.
2. We use the `method:` :get to override the default post.
3. The action is the destination URL.
4. The `form.submit` creates a button with the desired text, but doesn't pass anything to the server because we set name: `nil`.

Concept Leads to Code

```
# Original
<%= link_to "Show this item", item %>

# Same functionality with a short form that will display a button
<%= form_with url: item, method: :get do |form| %>
  <%= form.submit "Show this item", name: nil %>
<% end %>
```

Of course, we wouldn't want to do this on every page where a `link_to` exists. Instead, we would like to change it in one place and have it be reflected everywhere in the application. Rails has templates that create templates, and this is an example of a widely used aspect of computer science called **metaprogramming**. That is, programs that write programs. Rails uses this extensively. One example is the relationships (e.g.: `has_many`) we put into models. These methods create the other methods we can then call to access the related data. Ruby also has a `method_missing` method on all objects. If you call a method that doesn't (yet) exist on an object, that method can create it on the fly.

All of these keep our application DRY and allow for customization in one place. If you create templates in the `lib/templates/orb/scaffold` directory, all new views will be based on those meta-templates. In our example, we want to change the `link_to` to a form on the index page. We can see how the template will look after processing by the ERB processor. For example, the `<%%` will be translated to `<%`, an example of character escaping. We also see actual `<%=` that will run the associated Ruby code in the creation of the ERB template.

Concept Leads to Code

```
# lib/templates/erb/scaffold/index.html.erb.tt
<p style="color: green"><%%= notice %></p>

<h1><%= human_name.pluralize %></h1>

<div id="<%= plural_table_name %>">
  <%% @<%= plural_table_name %>.each do |<%= singular_table_name %>| %>
    <%%= render <%= singular_table_name %> %>
    <p%>
      <%%= form_with url: <%= model_resource_name(singular_table_name) %>,
method: :get do |form| %>
        <%%= form.submit "Show this <%= human_name.downcase %>", name: nil %>
      <%% end %>
    </p>
  <%% end %>
</div>

<%%= form_with url: <%= new_helper(type: :path) %>, method: :get do |form| %>
  <%%= form.submit "New <%= human_name.downcase %>", name: nil %>
<%% end %>
```

Cascading Style Sheets

An important concept in computing is the separation of concerns. For web applications, we use HTML for structure and content, *Cascading Style Sheets (CSS)* for appearance, and JavaScript for interactivity. We've already seen the separation of concerns concept in the MVC pattern for interactive applications. A database for the model, a widely used programming language for the controllers, and some form of interface for the view.

Rails comes with quite a few CSS frameworks that you can specify either in the `rails` new command, or by installing them later with `bundle install`.

- Tailwind CSS
- Bootstrap
- Bulma
- PostCSS, and
- Dart Sass

Tailwind CSS (https://tailwindcss.com/) is a popular framework that's easy to incorporate it into a Rails application to improve the *look and feel* of a Rails application. Another major upside to many of the CSS libraries is that they are **responsive**: they respond to the screen size of the device displaying the content. The page will look different on a large monitor versus a small phone. For example, menus will be displayed on high-resolution displays, but show as a "hamburger" that needs to be expanded on lower-resolution displays. These responsive CSS libraries are important to use as many of our applications should be mobile first to reflect the nature of the user's access.

Concept Leads to Code

```
rails new Todos --minimal --css=tailwind
cd Todos
rails tailwindcss:build
rails generate scaffold Item what:string when:date
rails db:migrate
rails server
```

On Demand or Just in Time

Another important concept in computing is **on-demand or Just in Time (JIT)** compilation or creation of executables or content.

While the above script will get you up and running with Tailwind CSS, when you make changes to the CSS it won't be reflected in the running application as the new CSS needs to be published via the asset pipeline. One approach would be to rebuild every time you make a change, but there is an easier way. We can have a process monitor all files related to a running application and have that process automatically rebuild the appropriate packages on demand or just in time. Many **continuous integration/continuous deployment (CI/CD)** systems do this. Software repositories monitor updates/commits and run a set of tests and deploy processes in response. The Tailwind CSS Gem comes with this capability in the form of foreman. Foreman looks at a `Procfile.dev` (dev for the development environment) that describes two processes to run: one the usual web server and the other `tailwindcss:watch`, the latter used to watch for CSS changes and rebuild the CSS delivered to the browser. To use this, you simply use **`./bin/dev`** instead of the usual **`rails server`**.

Another on-demand optimizer is a server pre-loader called Spring. It is no longer installed by default, due in large part to most computers having fast enough CPUs and disks but is available as a Gem. It must only be used in a development environment.

Zeitwerk (https://github.com/fxn/zeitwerk) is another on-demand optimizer that Rails 7 does use. It loads Ruby classes and modules when they are needed, not all at the beginning, saving time and memory space. Zeitwerk also automatically reloads Ruby classes or modules that change, allowing us to make changes in files and have those changes reflected in a running application.

There is also the *asset pipeline* that combines the static web content into a single file to reduce the number of requests a browser makes, thereby reducing the number of responses a server makes. The default asset pipeline for Rails is called Sprockets. Sprockets combines many different HTML, CSS, and JavaScript files, possibly performing optimizations, before sending the content to the browser. One typical optimization is minification: removing or reducing content that the browser doesn't need. The stripping of white space in files is typical. White space is very useful for developer readability, but it is not needed for browser consumption. Minification may also rename variables to make them shorter. Another possible optimization is reducing the amount of data sent by compression and GZIP compression is understood by most browsers. Here, we see a typical time/space tradeoff: we spend time on the server making the space of the sent content smaller. The browser then spends time reversing the process. Text can often be reduced by at least 50%, saving network transmission time. If the decrease in transmission time is less than the time spent compressing/decompressing the content, this can be a win. Of course, computing time here also means power consumption so in low-power environments or if concerns other than power consumption outweigh the increased speed, we might choose to not pay the increased power consumption cost.

An important aspect of the asset pipeline is the resources shared by all the pages. An example of this is found in `app/views/layouts/application.html.erb`. This file's contents are used by the pipeline as the overall layout for a site. Changes here are reflected on all pages and where we put items that we want shown on all pages such as search, navigation, etc. It uses the Ruby yield command to render the rest of any page.

Concept Leads to Code

```
<!DOCTYPE html>
<html>
  <head>
    <title>I18N</title>
    <meta name="viewport" content="width=device-width,initial-scale=1">
    <%= csrf_meta_tags %>
    <%= csp_meta_tag %>

    <%= stylesheet_link_tag "application" %>
  </head>

  <body>
    <%= yield %>
  </body>
</html>
```

Form Helpers

Rails has numerous ERB methods that help with the creation of forms. The basic helper is `form_with`. Here is a simple form to submit a text field to the server and the HTML output it produces for the browser.

Concept Leads to Code

```
# The following form helper:
<%= form_with(model: message) do |form| %>
  <div>
    <%= form.label :message, style: "display: block" %>
    <%= form.text_field :message %>
  </div>
  <div>
    <%= form.submit %>
  </div>
<% end %>

# Creates the following form:
<form action="/messages" accept-charset="UTF-8" method="post">
  <input type="hidden" name="authenticity_token"
    value="hp-Yixk9TkWMbywnlyZ5uPuslbnqy2_KXhBqeqtj233amEl-
I8vnhNwTYKrTT9Dh8HDhjI_hmwVwhLeIWdIFMw"
    autocomplete="off" />

  <div>
    <label style="display: block" for="message_message">Message</label>
    <input type="text" name="message[message]" id="message_message" />
  </div>

  <div>
    <input type="submit" name="commit" value="Create Message"
      data-disable-with="Create Message" />
  </div>
</form>
```

The `authenticity_token` is used to reduce the possibility of Cross-Site Request Forgeries, adding to the security of your web application. Rails checks that when you submit the form, the `authenticity_token` it sent in the form is the one that is associated with the submission. We'll cover this and other Rails security measures in the chapter on security. The `data-disable-with` disables the submit button after a click to keep the user from clicking multiple times and possibly disrupting the communication between the client and server.

Here are some of the helpers for various types of input fields.

- `check_box`
- `radio_button`
- `text_area`

- `hidden_field`
- `password_field`
- `number_field`
- `range_field`
- `date_field`
- `time_field`
- `datetime_local_field`
- `month_field`
- `week_field`
- `search_field`
- `email_field`
- `telephone_field`
- `url_field`
- `color_field`

A number of these have HTML5 controls to help the user choose valid values.

Collection Helpers

In addition to the single-field helpers above, Rails provides helpers that allow you to choose from a collection.

1. `collection_check_boxes`

Creates a set of check boxes for choosing one or more values.

1. `collection_radio_buttons`

Creates a set of radio buttons for selecting one value.

1. `collection_select`

Creates a drop-down for selecting one value.

Each of these take the same arguments `method, collection, value_method, text_method, options = {}, html_options = {}, &block`. The `method` is called to set the value in the model. The `collection` is the collection that contains all the possible values. The `value_method` is the method called on each member of the collection to get the value to be assigned to the method on form submission. The `text_method` is the method called to display the values to select in a human-readable form. There are a wide variety of options and `html_options` that can be specified via hashes. Finally, you can optionally pass a block in for an even greater degree of customization.

For example, if a student `has_one` advisor, the following will create a drop-down to choose an advisor for a specific student **`<%= form.collection_select :advisor_id, Advisor.all, :id, :name %>`**. If an advisor `has_many` students, the following will create checkboxes to assign students to an advisor**`<%= form.collection_check_boxes :student_ids, Student.all, :id, :name %>`**. Note, for the `has_many` relationship, you will need to modify the require/permit arguments in the controller to allow passing an array of values, along the lines of **`params.require(:advisor).permit(:name, student_ids: [])`**.

Another wrinkle is if you want to display more than one field in the collection helper. An easy way is to define a method in the model that returns the appropriate string and pass that in as the text_method.

Concept Leads to Code

```
# app/models/student.rb
class Student < ApplicationRecord
  belongs_to :advisor

  def full_name
    "#{first_name} #{last_name}"
  end
end

# app/views/advisors/_form.html.erb
  <div>
    <%= form.label :full_name, style: "display: block" %>
    <%= form.collection_check_boxes :student_ids, Student.all, :id, :full_name %>
  </div>
```

Dynamic View Updates

Rails comes with Action Cable that is layered on top of web sockets. Web sockets form a persistent connection between a web client and server, unlike the usual request/response cycle. This allows for the dynamic updating of views that make for highly interactive applications. Rails 7 includes Hotwire (https://hotwired.dev/) and specifically Turbo (https://turbo.hotwired.dev/) that uses *HTTP over the wire* instead of making JSON requests. This allows, with very few lines of code, the ability to update views without the overhead of creating web sockets or continuously calling **JSON APIs**. Let's create a messaging application where users can communicate with each other on an ongoing basis. We can create the basis via our usual **`rails generate scaffold Message message:string`**. We then need to modify only two files, the view, and the model, to make the application respond dynamically to the addition/deletion/modification of messages.

Concept Leads to Code

```
# app/models/message.rb
class Message < ApplicationRecord
  after_create_commit { broadcast_append_to "messages" }
  after_update_commit { broadcast_update_to "messages" }
  after_destroy_commit { broadcast_remove_to "messages" }
end

# app/views/messages/index.html.erb
<p style="color: green"><%= notice %></p>
<h1>Messages</h1>
<%= turbo_stream_from "messages" %>
<div id="messages">
  <% @messages.each do |message| %>
    <%= render message %>
    <p>
      <%= link_to "Show this message", message %>
    </p>
  <% end %>
</div>
<%= link_to "New message", new_message_path %>
```

That's it. The model is given the channel (`messages` in this case) to send updates to when a message is created, updated, or destroyed. The view adds a single line to subscribe to the channel via a Turbo stream so that the display is always up to date. These few changes make a simple real-time messaging system.

JSON APIs

Application Programming Interfaces

We write *Application Programming Interfaces (APIs)* all the time. All the public methods in our classes create an API that other programmers can call. Documenting all our APIs, including our public methods, adds greatly to their reusability. Ruby has RDoc (https://github.com/ruby/rdoc) and there are semi-automated approaches to creating JSON API documentation for our Rails servers.

As the servers we write may often, or even exclusively, be used by alternative (non-Rails or non-HTML) frontends (Rails recognizes this with the<span class="import-Code" –api argument to the new command), having formal versioning and description of our APIs allows clients to discover and correctly use our APIs.

Versioning

As our applications evolve, we need to change version numbers so our clients are aware of the features of the current application. A popular approach to *versioning* is called *Semantic Versioning* (see: https://semver.org/). The following points are from that website.

- MAJOR version when you make incompatible API changes.
    - That is, users of an existing API cannot use the new version without rewriting some of their code.
- MINOR version when you add functionality in a backward-compatible manner.
    - Here, existing client code continues to work, but there is new functionality that requires client code to be modified.
- PATCH version when you make backward-compatible bug fixes.
    - For this, the only visible change is that one or more fixes are made, and clients shouldn't have to rewrite any of their code unless they created workarounds for the bugs.

There are many other recommendations on the above website that are well worth following.

It is important to communicate API version numbers and there are several different approaches. A popular approach is to specify the version number directly in the URL. Another is to specify it in a query parameter. Regardless, this allows for servers to run more than one version of an API and respond appropriately to client requests.

Ajax

Another important aspect of web applications is interacting with JavaScript frontends and other web applications directly. There have been many approaches to this through the years including exposing data via the *eXtensible Markup Language (XML)* and *SOAP (aka Simple Object Access Protocol)*. These days, the *JavaScript Object Notation (JSON)* language has become the dominant approach. Happily, Rails provides this interface by default using the JBuilder gem. JBuilder supplies a Domain-Specific Language (DSL) to create JSON from the models of an application. It is an alternative view to HTML. You can recognize the view files that provide this interface via their `json.jbuilder` suffix; each is a template in a DSL just as ERBs are.

If you want to use `-minimal` to build a rails app, but want to use JBuilder, do `bundle add jbuilder` before creating any views, including views that are part of a scaffold.

These days, most API clients rely on *Ajax*. This originally stood for *Asynchronous JavaScript And XML (AJAX)*, but these days as we don't use XML as much we call it simply Ajax. Asynchronous because the early web required submission to a server, either via clicking a link or submitting a form, for a page to change. Now, many events can autonomously, and asynchronously, send and receive data from a server and update a page in real time. Events such as keypresses, hovering over an element, etc., can send and receive data and this is the expectation of users. Rails has an HTTP-over-the-wire approach built in and supports asynchronous JSON queries and responses.

Domain-Specific Languages

Domain-Specific Languages (DSLs) are used, as their name implies, to address a specific domain of computing. They are not general-purpose languages, as Ruby is. We've already seen several DSLs: HTML, CSS, and ERB. HTML expresses web page contents and their relationship to each other, and CSS expresses how web pages are styled (fonts, colors, etc.) Neither is what is called Turing complete, a term used to describe languages that compute anything computable. Instead, they express part of an application in a language that is targeted to a specific aspect of the overall application. They are typically much smaller (and less expressive) than a general-purpose language. Their power exists in their specificity to a particular problem domain. JBuilder allows us to create terse descriptions of what data are exposed in a JSON API.

There are several useful methods in JBuilder, most of which end with !. When a call is made that doesn't match an existing JBuilder method, `method_missing` is of course called. This examines the name of the called method and uses that name as a field of the current model and extracts that value and formats it in JSON. Two JBuilder methods that Rails uses are the following.

- `json.array!`

  This method iterates through a collection, typically passing each member to a partial.

- `json.extract!`

  Receives an object and a list of fields and formats each in JSON.

  We see all of these methods, including the `method_missing`, in the code below.

Concept Leads to Code

```
# app/views/todos/index.json.jbuilder
json.array! @todos, partial: "todos/todo", as: :todo

# app/views/todos/_todo.json.jbuilder
json.extract! todo, :id, :item, :due, :created_at, :updated_at
json.url todo_url(todo, format: :json)
```

The `index.json.jbuilder` iterates through a collection, passing each to a `todo` partial. The extract! in the `_todo.json.jbuilder` partial then extracts various fields in the object and formats them in JSON. The `json.url` doesn't match a method in JBuilder so `method_missing` is called, and the key/value pair is formatted in valid JSON.

Surfing to `http://localhost:3000/todos/2.json` will give a JSON object for a single todo, and surfing to `http://localhost:3000/todos.json` will produce an array of all the todos.

Concept Leads to Code

```
# http://localhost:3000/todos/2.json
{"id":2,"item":"Learn about
JBuilder","due":"2023-02-28","created_at":"2023-02-28T18:12:44.767Z","updated_at"
:"2023-02-28T18:12:44.767Z","url":"http://localhost:3000/todos/2.json"}
# http://localhost:3000/todos.json
[{"id":2,"item":"Learn about
JBuilder","due":"2023-02-28","created_at":"2023-02-28T18:12:44.767Z","updated_at"
:"2023-02-28T18:12:44.767Z","url":"http://localhost:3000/todos/2.json"},
{"id":3,"item":"Write about
JBuilder","due":"2023-02-28","created_at":"2023-02-28T18:12:58.969Z","updated_at"
:"2023-02-28T18:12:58.969Z","url":"http://localhost:3000/todos/3.json"}]
```

Note that Rails will create a JSON API default, so if you don't want that exposed you should use the `-no-api` to `rails new`.

Documenting APIs

Once we have created a JSON API, it is a good idea to document it so that clients can know what is available. Two methods for doing this are OpenAPI and GraphQL, and Rails supports both. This allows clients to query a web resource to find what endpoints/resources are available, find the parameter and return types, etc.

OpenAPI

OpenAPI (https://www.openapis.org/) is a widely used DSL that is used to describe the capabilities of APIs. It is an evolution of the Swagger Specification; Swagger continues to support an extensive toolchain for the specification, development, publishing, and display of APIs (https://swagger.io/). There is a gem named `rswag` that helps when creating an OpenAPI implementation for a Rails server (https://github.com/rswag/rswag). It extends the `rspec-rails` *Behavior Driven Development* (*BDD*, https://en.wikipedia.org/wiki/Behavior-driven_development) gem and its DSL for describing and testing APIs.

Concept Leads to Code

```
rails new OpenAPI --api
cd OpenAPI/
rails generate scaffold Item what when:date
rails db:migrate

bundle add rswag
rails generate rswag:install

bundle add rspec
bundle add 'rspec-rails'
rails generate rspec:install

# Create the initial specification from the item object
rails generate rspec:swagger items
# Rerun this after every modification to spec directory
rails rswag:specs:swaggerize                # Or rails rswag
# Surf to http://localhost:3000/api-docs/index.html
# In spec/requests/items_spec.rb
  path '/items/{id}' do
    parameter name: 'id', in: :path, type: :string, description: 'id'
    parameter name: :item, in: :body, schema: {
      type: :object,
      properties: {
        what: { type: :string },
        when: { type: :string, format: :date}
      },
      required: ['what', 'when']
    }
```

By default, a YAML file is dynamically created and can be fetched to use the API. We can change the two instances of `yaml` to `json` in `spec/swagger_helper.rb` to also expose a JSON endpoint. We can directly fetch either via curl as the following demonstrates.

Concept Leads to Code

```
curl http://localhost:3000/api-docs/v1/swagger.yaml

curl http://localhost:3000/api-docs/v1/swagger.json
```

Graph Query Language (GraphQL)

GraphQL (https://graphql.org/) is another approach to documenting and interacting with APIs. It supports reading, mutating, and possibly subscribing to exposed API calls. It typically has a single endpoint for all operations but allows the client to specify what exact data they are interested in retrieving. This contrasts with other API implementations that have multiple endpoints that are used to customize the data returned. For Rails, there is a gem that is a great help in implementing GraphQL (https://graphql-ruby.org/). Let's start with our typical application.

Concept Leads to Code

```
rails new Todo --minimal
cd Todo
rails generate scaffold Item what when:date
rails db:migrate
curl https://drb80.github.io/WebAppDev/SeedFiles/lorem.rb > db/seeds.rb
rails db:seed
```

Now, let's add the `graphql` gem, install it, and generate the files needed to expose our Items.

Concept Leads to Code

```
bundle add graphql
rails generate graphql:install
rails generate graphql:object Item
```

Nicely, this gem also installs a web interface that we can use to run GraphQL queries; it is at the /graphiql route for our application.

Concept Leads to Code

```
# config/routes.rb
Rails.application.routes.draw do
  if Rails.env.development?
    mount GraphiQL::Rails::Engine, at: "/graphiql", graphql_path: "/graphql"
  end
  post "/graphql", to: "graphql#execute"
  resources :items
end
```

During development only, we might want to disable cross-site request forgery protection (CSRF). In general, for production, **this is a very bad idea**. There is one line near the top of `app/controllers/graphql_controller.rb` that can be changed to turn off CSRF protecting in development.

Concept Leads to Code

```
protect_from_forgery with: :null_session if Rails.env.development?
```

With this in place, a simple test can be run with the boilerplate the graphql gem provides.

Concept Leads to Code

```
curl 'http://localhost:3000/graphql' --json '{"query":"{testField{}}"}'
=> {"data":{"testField":"Hello World!"}}
```

The **`rails generate graphql:object Item`** above creates a type file from the model and in this case, places it in `app/graphql/types/item_type.rb`.

Concept Leads to Code

```
module Types
  class ItemType < Types::BaseObject
    field :id, ID, null: false
    field :what, String
    field :when, GraphQL::Types::ISO8601Date
    field :created_at, GraphQL::Types::ISO8601DateTime, null: false
    field :updated_at, GraphQL::Types::ISO8601DateTime, null: false
  end
end
```

The final task is to describe the API endpoints we want to expose. This is done in the `app/graphql/types/query_type.rb` file. Here, we expose retrieving both a single item and all the items. It uses the type defined above; in one case it returns one item, and in another an array of items. Along with being able to query, the field can describe what is returned; how many arguments there are, their types, if they are required, etc. There are many other descriptors of course, and you can describe mutators and subscriptions.

Concept Leads to Code

```
field :item, Types::ItemType, null: false,
  description: "An item" do
  argument :id, Int, required: true
end

def item(id:)
  Item.find(id)
end

field :items, [Types::ItemType], null: false,
  description: "A list of items"

def items
  Item.all
end
```

Start the Rails server and go to http://localhost:3000/graphiql to see the web interface of the GraphQL engine. You can also use Postman, curl, etc. as the following demonstrates.

Concept Leads to Code

```
# All the item identifiers
curl 'http://localhost:3000/graphql' --json '{"query":"{items{id}}"}'
{"data":{"items":[{"id":"21"},{"id":"22"},{"id":"23"},{"id":"24"},{"id":"25"},{"i
d":"26"},{"id":"27"},{"id":"28"},{"id":"29"},{"id":"30"}]}}
# All the todo's and nothing else
curl 'http://localhost:3000/graphql' --json '{"query":"{items{what}}"}'
{"data":{"items":[{"what":"Duvel"},{"what":"Shakespeare Oatmeal"},{"what":"St.
Bernardus Abt 12"},{"what":"Delirium Tremens"},{"what":"Schneider
Aventinus"},{"what":"Bourbon County Stout"},{"what":"Chocolate
St"},{"what":"Hercules Double IPA"},{"what":"Brooklyn Black"},{"what":"Delirium
Noctorum"}]}}
# All the created_at's and nothing else
curl 'http://localhost:3000/graphql' --json '{"query":"{items{createdAt}}"}'
{"data":{"items":[{"createdAt":"2023-12-25T04:15:13Z"},{"createdAt":"2023-12-25T0
4:15:13Z"},{"createdAt":"2023-12-25T04:15:13Z"},{"createdAt":"2023-12-25T04:15:13
Z"},{"createdAt":"2023-12-25T04:15:13Z"},{"createdAt":"2023-12-25T04:15:13Z"},{"c
reatedAt":"2023-12-25T04:15:13Z"},{"createdAt":"2023-12-25T04:15:13Z"},{"createdA
t":"2023-12-25T04:15:13Z"},{"createdAt":"2023-12-25T04:15:13Z"}]}}
# A specific todo
curl 'http://localhost:3000/graphql' --json '{"query":"{item (id:21){what}}"}'
{"data":{"item":{"what":"Duvel"}}}
# Ask for the overall schema, not recommended to be publicly available
curl 'http://localhost:3000/graphql' --json '{"query":"{__schema{types{name
fields{name}}}}"}'
# Part of what comes back:
{"name":"Item",
  "fields":
    [
      {"name":"createdAt"},
      {"name":"id"},
      {"name":"updatedAt"},
      {"name":"what"},
      {"name":"when"}
    ]
},
{"name":"Query",
  "fields":
    [
      {"name":"item"},
      {"name":"items"},
    ]
},
```

JavaScript Browser Frameworks

There are many good *JavaScript* (strictly speaking *ECMAScript*, but we'll use the typical terminology here) frameworks that create compelling user experiences. While Ruby and JavaScript have different histories, they share many similarities, and knowing one helps with learning the other. Both include the following.

1. Very object-oriented. All variables and constants are references, and all references refer to objects.
2. Interpreted, at least as a paradigm. This means both are dynamic, allowing the addition of methods and data to existing objects and classes at runtime.
3. Ruby has class-based inheritance, while JavaScript has prototypical inheritance but has added syntax to reflect many users' experiences with class-based inheritance.
4. Ruby uses duck typing, while JavaScript is weakly typed. Duck typing states if I have a reference to an object and it has a method that does what I want, that object is type-compatible. That is "if it walks like a duck and quacks like a duck, it's a duck." For example, an integer that has a + method can receive a float as an argument, the expression `1.+(1.0)` (call the + method on the integer 1 with a parameter of 1.0) results in 2.0. Equivalent expressions include `1.+1.0` and `1 + 1.0` as the elision of parentheses is allowed in Ruby. JavaScript has similar abilities but adds type coercion, so that `"1" + 1.0` results in `"11"` where this is an error in Ruby. In JavaScript, the 1.0 is coerced to a string and then string concatenation is then performed.

TypeScript (a typed version of JavaScript) also has many good browser frameworks available.

The Document Object Model

When a browser downloads a web resource, it places the resulting document into a tree data structure called the *Document Object Model (DOM)*. As a well-formed HTML document has all its elements properly nested, the tree is well-formed and can easily be traversed. Browsers tend to be somewhat forgiving on the HTML they accept and still create a valid DOM. For all the details on HTML5, building the tree, etc., see https://html.spec.whatwg.org/. The tree contains all the information from a web resource including the HTML elements and attributes, the CSS declarations, etc. Anything that is in an HTML or CSS element can be changed, deleted, or added to. There are JavaScript methods for traversing the DOM or for finding specific nodes in the DOM.

This capability of being able to modify a page in place leads to the creation of more native-looking web applications. One approach is called a *Single-Page Application (SPA)*. These are similar to traditional web applications, but instead of moving from page to page for functionality, SPAs stay on the same page and interact with the server asynchronously. Many web applications are designed this way and can look very much like traditional desktop applications, albeit within a web browser.

Another approach is called a *Progressive Web Application (PWA)*. Here, progressive denotes that as the application gains more access to native hardware resources (the file system, camera, etc.), the more it will utilize those resources. While PWAs run inside a browser's environment, the usual browser window with menus and tabs isn't shown and instead only what is defined by the PWA appears. PWAs do require some additional components, such as service workers.

Both SPAs and PWAs can allow for offline work and are automatically updated on an ongoing basis as they are delivered from a web server. Another benefit is when we use more than one either, they can share a single instance of the underlying browser, saving resources compared to stand-alone, native applications. Additionally, both run wherever the browser does, making the creation of cross-platform applications substantially easier.

Yet another approach is taken by Electron (https://www.electronjs.org/), and similarly Microsoft's WebView2 (https://developer.microsoft.com/en-us/microsoft-edge/webview2/). Here, not only is the HTML/

CSS/JavaScript bundled together, but a browser is also included in the bundle. This also allows for a native application-like experience, and it is independent of having a particular browser installed. Downsides versus a PWA include the following.

1. A much larger installation package as the underlying browser is included in the installation. This may also lead to longer load times.
2. The need to update the entire package including the underlying browser when necessary, instead of only the parts that change from release to release.

Vue.js

Vue.js (in the following examples, version 2 (https://v2.vuejs.org/) but note there is a more recent version 3 (https://vuejs.org/)) is a popular JavaScript browser framework that uses the *Model-View-ViewModel (MVVM)* paradigm. In essence, MVVM presents the state of relevant data to the user via displaying JavaScript variables. Vue maps this state to the DOM and uses *two-way binding* to both display and update the state. Vue uses the separation of concerns approach by not intermingling JavaScript and HTML. Vue typically uses element references in JavaScript and uses *mustaches* (double curly brackets) to display the state of JavaScript variables. Vue allows us to abstract away from DOM details such as event handlers and focus on declaring how data are modified and displayed. Here is a simple script that demonstrates the two-way binding of an input field to a JavaScript variable.

Concept Leads to Code

```
<!DOCTYPE html>
<html>
  <head>
    <title>Vue Two-way Binding</title>
    <script src="https://cdn.jsdelivr.net/npm/vue@2/dist/vue.js"></script>
  </head>
  <body>
    <!-- Set aside a div to reference from Vue -->
    <div id="two-way">
      <!-- A mustache that displays the datum as it is modified -->
      <p>{{ message }}</p>
      <!-- A Vue reference to the model below -->
      <input v-model="message">
    </div>

    <script type="text/javascript">
      const App = new Vue({
        // The name of the shared element
        el: '#two-way',
        // The data and an initial message
        data: { message: 'WebAppDev' }
    })
    </script>
  </body>
</html>
```

You can save this file and open it directly in your browser to experiment with two-way binding. You can also open the browser console and enter **`App.message = "Hello World!"`** to see that modifications to the JavaScript variable are reflected in the DOM.

Here is a simple Vue.js script that interacts with our JSON todo API.

Concept Leads to Code

```
<!DOCTYPE html>
<html>
  <head>
    <title>A Todo SPA</title>
    <!-- Pull in the Vue package -->
    <script src="https://cdn.jsdelivr.net/npm/vue@2/dist/vue.js"></script>
  </head>

  <body>
    <div id="Itemlist">
      <ul>
      <!-- A Vue for loop -->
      <li v-for="item in items">
        <!-- A Vue delete click event handler -->
        <button v-on:click="deleteItem(item.id)">Done!</button>
        <!-- Vue mustashes -->
        {{item.when}} {{item.what}}
      </li>
      </ul>

      <!-- A Vue submit click event handler -->
      <form v-on:submit="newItem">
        <div>
          <label for="what">What: </label>
          <input id="what" type="text">
          <label for="when">When: </label>
          <input id="when" type="date">
          <input type="submit" value="New">
        </div>
      </form>
    </div>

    <script type="text/javascript">
      new Vue({
        // The element id from above.
        el: '#Itemlist',
        // The data displayed in the v-for loop above.
        data: { items: [] },
        methods: {
          // Grab all the items from the JSON API
          showItems: function() {
            fetch('http://localhost:3000/items.json')
              .then(response => response.json()
                .then(json => { this.items = json; }))
                .catch(error => { console.log(error); })
```

```
            .catch(error => { console.log(error); })
        },
        // Delete one item via the JSON API
        deleteItem: function(id) {
          fetch('http://localhost:3000/items/' + id + '.json',
            {method: 'DELETE'})
              .then(this.showItems)
              .catch(error => { console.log(error); })
            },
        // Create one item via the JSON API
        newItem: function(e) {
          // Don't submit the usual way.
          e.preventDefault()
          // Grab the data from the form.
          data = {what: e.target.elements.what.value,
            when: e.target.elements.when.value}
          // Submit via JSON.
          fetch('http://localhost:3000/items.json', {
            method: 'POST',
            headers: { "Content-Type": "application/json" },
            body: JSON.stringify(data),
          })
            .then(this.showItems)
            .catch(error => { console.log(error); })
        },
      },
      // The first thing to do.
      mounted: function() {
        this.showItems()
      },
    })
    </script>
  </body>
</html>
```

You can directly save and open the above file or save the file as index.html and start a very simple Rails server such as the following.

Concept Leads to Code

```
gem install webrick
ruby -run -ehttpd . -p8000
```

In either case, make sure there is a JSON todo API running on port 3000. For the webrick case, surf to `http://localhost:8000` to see the results.

React

React is a popular frontend framework that takes a different approach from Vue. It interleaves JavaScript and HTML, implying that those who write the code for an application are also often in charge of the user interface. While this removes the separation of concerns paradigm, it may reflect the nature of web application development. Indeed, *full-stack* developers work from the database to the user interface daily. With React, we create reusable components in JavaScript, each of which returns a form of HTML called JSX (approximately JavaScript XML).

JSX is independent of React and other frameworks support it. JSX is stricter than usual HTML. Here are a few of the rules we must follow.

- Each JavaScript component can only return a single HTML element. We can surround what we return by a `<div>`, or a `<Fragment>` (there is a shortcut for a `<Fragment>: <>`).
- All elements must be closed. For example, image elements must be in the form of `<img />`.
- Because `class` is a reserved word in JavaScript, we must use `className` in elements.
- We can add JavaScript expressions to JSX but note that JavaScript statements are not allowed.

There are some *hooks* (points of dependence injection) that React provides. Here are two we will use in the following example.

- `useState`
    - Create a React variable with an initial value and a mutator that React controls.
- `useEffect`
    - Responds to external events; we'll use here to respond to render events.

The following is similar to the Vue example above, but only displays the items and does not add or remove them.

Concept Leads to Code

```
<!DOCTYPE html>
<html>
  <head>
    <meta charset="UTF-8" />
    <title>Todos</title>
    <script src="https://unpkg.com/react@18/umd/react.development.js"></script>
    <script src="https://unpkg.com/react-dom@18/umd/react-
dom.development.js"></script>
    <script src="https://unpkg.com/@babel/standalone/babel.min.js"></script>
  </head>
  <body>
    <!-- This is all the HTML there is, React does everything else. -->
    <div id="root"></div>

    <script type="text/babel">
      function MyApp() {
```

```
        // Set aside the data and the mutator, and set the initial state
        const [items, setItems] = React.useState(null);

        // Call every time a render occurs
        React.useEffect(() => {
          const getItems = async () => {
            // Use ES6's fetch
            const b = await fetch('http://localhost:3000/items.json');
            const c = await b.json();
            // Call the mutator from above
            setItems(c);
          }
          // Call what we just defined
          getItems();
        // An empty array denotes only the first render
        }, []);

        // One table datum
        function tableItem(item) {
          return (
            <>
              <td>{item.what}</td>
              <td>{item.when}</td>
            </>
          );
        }

        // Create a row and call the previous method
        function tableRow(item) {
          return (
            <tr key={item.id}>
              { tableItem(item) }
            </tr>
          );
        }

        // Iterate through all the data using map
        return (
          <table border="1">
            <tbody>
              { items && items.map(item => tableRow(item)) }
            </tbody>
          </table>
        );
      }

      // Reference the identifier we set above
      const container = document.getElementById('root');
      const root = ReactDOM.createRoot(container);
      root.render(<MyApp />);
    </script>
  </body>
</html>
```

React Native

React Native (https://reactnative.dev/) is a cross-platform framework that has native extensions for iOS and Android phones and tablets. This allows us to create applications using JavaScript/HTML/CSS that run as if they're native. React Native includes abstractions for the following.

- View—a rectangular container, a `<div>` in HTML parlance.
- Text—displays styled text, a `<p>`.
- Image—an `<img>`.
- ScrollView—a scrollable `<div>` that can contain multiple components.
- TextInput—an `<input>` form element.

Probably the easiest way to start experimenting with React Native is to surf to https://snack.expo.dev and replace the App.js file with the following, which is quite similar to the React application above but with React Native extensions. Again, make sure you have a Todo API running on port 3000.

Concept Leads to Code

```
import React, { useEffect, useState } from 'react'
import { ScrollView } from 'react-native'

// Create a set of components using properties
const Items = props => {
  // useState is a hook to create a variable React monitors. We call the
  // mutator setData, and the initial value of the variable is null.
  const [data, setData] = React.useState(null)

  React.useEffect(() => {
    const getData = async () => {
      // Use ES6's fetch
      const b = await fetch('http://localhost:3000/items.json')
      const c = await b.json()
      // Call the setData method from the useState hook
      setData(c)
    }
    getData()
  // The empty array denotes calling only once
  }, [])

  // One table datum
  function tableData (item) {
    return (
      <>
        <td>{item.what}</td>
        <td>{item.when}</td>
      </>
    )
  }

  // Create a row and call the previous method
```

```
    function tableRow (item) {
      return (
        <tr key={item.id}>
          { tableData(item) }
        </tr>
      )
    }

    // Iterate though all the data using map
    return (
      <table border="1px">
        <tbody>
          { data && data.map(item => tableRow(item)) }
        </tbody>
      </table>
    )
  }

  // Call the above components
  const App = () => {
    return (
      <ScrollView>
        <Items/>
      </ScrollView>
    )
  }

  export default App
```

You can also set up a local development environment using the following. You'll first need *Node.js* (https://nodejs.org/en) installed.

Concept Leads to Code

```
npx create-expo-app ReactNativeTodo
cd ReactNativeTodo
npx expo install react-native-web react-dom @expo/metro-runtime
# Edit App.js to reflect the script above
npm run web
```

Electron

Electron Web Application

Electron (https://www.electronjs.org) is another approach to front-ending a web application. It uses both Node (https://nodejs.org/) and Chromium (https://www.chromium.org/Home/) to create a native application that runs on the three major operating systems. End users cannot tell the difference between an Electron application and one that was written specifically for the operating system. This is because Node has access to the operating system calls and therefore exposes the native user interface to end users. Here are some of the native interfaces included in Electron.

- clipboard
- dialog
- Menu
- Notification
- screen
- session
- shell
- systemPreferences

It is relatively straightforward to create a simple Electron app. First, create a directory and place the `index.html` file from the Vue application above there. You'll then need a main.js file that creates an Electron window and loads the Vue `index.html` file into that window. There is also a developer tools window that is useful during development.

Concept Leads to Code

```
# main.js
const { app, BrowserWindow } = require('electron')
const createWindow = () => {
  const mainWindow = new BrowserWindow({
    width: 800,
    height: 600
  })
  mainWindow.loadFile('index.html')
  // Open the developer toolbox
  mainWindow.webContents.openDevTools()
}
app.whenReady().then(() => {
  createWindow()
  app.on('activate', () => {
    if (BrowserWindow.getAllWindows().length === 0) createWindow()
  })
})
app.on('window-all-closed', () => {
  if (process.platform !== 'darwin') app.quit()
})
```

Now we need to initialize the folder so that Node packages can be installed. The *Node Package Manager (npm)* can be used for this. This utility will walk you through creating a `package.json` file. It only covers the most common items and tries to guess sensible defaults.

Concept Leads to Code

```
npm init
See `npm help init` for definitive documentation on these fields and exactly
what they do.
Use `npm install <pkg>` afterwards to install a package and save it as a
dependency in the package.json file.
Press ^C at any time to quit.
package name: (todo)
version: (1.0.0)
description: An Electron frontend to a todo API
entry point: (index.js) main.js
test command: exit 1
git repository:
keywords:
author: Steve Beaty
license: (ISC) MIT
About to write to /private/tmp/Todo/package.json:

{
  "name": "todo",
  "version": "1.0.0",
  "description": "An Electron frontend to a todo API",
  "main": "main.js",
  "scripts": {
    "test": "exit 1"
  },
  "author": "Steve Beaty",
  "license": "MIT"
}

Is this OK? (yes)
```

Now we can add the Node packages needed for Electron.

Concept Leads to Code

```
npm install --save-dev electron
added 77 packages, and audited 78 packages in 18s
21 packages are looking for funding
  run `npm fund` for details
found 0 vulnerabilities
npm install --save-dev @electron-forge/cli
added 371 packages, and audited 449 packages in 10s
66 packages are looking for funding
  run `npm fund` for details
found 0 vulnerabilities
npx electron-forge import
✓ Checking your system
✓ Locating importable project
✓ Processing configuration and dependencies
  ✓ Installing dependencies
  ✓ Copying base template Forge configuration
  ✓ Fixing .gitignore
✓ Finalizing import
› We have attempted to convert your app to be in a format that Electron F…
  Thanks for using Electron Forge!
# Currently needed.
npm install --save-dev '@electron-forge/plugin-fuses'
added 5 packages, and audited 511 packages in 2s
68 packages are looking for funding
  run `npm fund` for details
found 0 vulnerabilities
```

At this point, we're ready to go. Start a todo server on port 3000 as before and start Electron.

Concept Leads to Code

```
npm start
> todo@1.0.0 start
> electron-forge start
✓ Checking your system
✓ Locating application
✓ Loading configuration
✓ Preparing native dependencies [0.7s]
✓ Running generateAssets hook
```

Once this works, we can make our standalone executable.

Concept Leads to Code

```
npm run make
> todo@1.0.0 make
> electron-forge make

✔ Checking your system
✔ Loading configuration
✔ Resolving make targets
  › Making for the following targets:
[...]
✔ Making distributables
  ✔ Making a zip distributable for darwin/arm64 [8s]
✔ Running postMake hook
  › Artifacts available at: /private/tmp/Todo/out/make
```

On a Mac, the executable can be run directly via `open out/todo-darwin-arm64/todo.app/Contents/MacOS/todo` and other platforms will have similar paths.

Electron Native Application

As Node.js has access to native operating system calls, pretty much anything we can do in a native application we can do in Electron. We can create a very simple application that asks the OS access to display the type of CPU an *Electron Native* application is running on. We'll use a Node package that retrieves this information (https://www.npmjs.com/package/systeminformation). We'll need to install it `npm install -save-dev systeminformation`.

A little background in Electron's architecture is in order. There is a main process that has access to the OS and creates the initial windows etc. Each window however does not have access to the OS and runs in a sandbox for security. Electron windows can call renderer processes that can communicate to the main process via *inter-process communication (IPC)*. That IPC must be set up via *channels* before windows are created. The main process, in conjunction with a preload script, can expose IPC endpoints to the renderer processes. Here is an example of a preload script and a main process that waits for a call once the window is rendered.

Concept Leads to Code

```
# preload.js
const { contextBridge, ipcRenderer } = require('electron/renderer')

contextBridge.exposeInMainWorld('electronAPI', {
  cpuBrand: () => ipcRenderer.invoke('cpuBrand')
})

# main.js
const { app, BrowserWindow, ipcMain } = require('electron/main')
const path = require('node:path')
const si = require('systeminformation')
```

```
// Return the CPU brand from systeminformation
async function cpuBrand () {
  const b = await si.cpu()
  return b.brand
}

function createWindow () {
  mainWindow = new BrowserWindow({
    webPreferences: {
      preload: path.join(__dirname, 'preload.js')
    }
  })
  mainWindow.loadFile('index.html')
  mainWindow.openDevTools()
}

app.whenReady().then(() => {
  // Set up receiving the interprocess communication message that needs to
  // run in main. Call the method above when received.
  ipcMain.handle('cpuBrand', cpuBrand)
  createWindow()
  app.on('activate', function () {
    if (BrowserWindow.getAllWindows().length === 0) createWindow()
  })
})

app.on('window-all-closed', function () {
  if (process.platform !== 'darwin') app.quit()
})

# renderer.js, called from index.html
// Wait for the page to be loaded and then set the CPU brand.
document.addEventListener('DOMContentLoaded', pageLoaded)

async function pageLoaded(){
  const cpuBrand = await window.electronAPI.cpuBrand()
  const cpuBrandElement = document.getElementById('cpuBrand')
  cpuBrandElement.innerText = cpuBrand
}

# index.html
<!DOCTYPE html>
<html>
  <head>
    <meta charset="UTF-8">
    <!-- https://developer.mozilla.org/en-US/docs/Web/HTTP/CSP -->
    <meta http-equiv="Content-Security-Policy" content="default-src 'self';
script-src 'self'">
    <title>Get the CPU Version</title>
  </head>
  <body>
    CPU Brand: <strong id="cpuBrand"></strong>
    <script src='./renderer.js'></script>
  </body>
</html>
```

Putting these files into place and running the npm and npx commands we ran above for the web application will create an application that accesses the OS and displays the CPU brand.

Summary

We've introduced how backend data are displayed to users, a critical component to all successful web applications. There are plenty of sites where the data tell a compelling story for users, but the interface fails to capitalize on that story. A good web application not only contains the data users want but also displays them in captivating ways. Rails approaches this, and the need to keep our applications DRY, via helpers, partials, rich text, and the dynamic updating of content. Rails can also create JSON APIs so that any web browser framework can create SPAs or PWAs in addition to the HTML provided by our Rails servers. Both SPAs and PWAs provide a more native-like experience with the benefits of cross-platform portability and continuous updating.

Exercises

Directions: Use what you learned in this chapter to complete the following tasks and exercises.

1. Create a user interface (probably a SPA) using a JavaScript browser framework that calls your Rails API. Current popular examples in addition to Vue.js and React include Angular (https://angular.io/), and Svelte (https://svelte.dev/), but there are many others.
2. Create an application that uses Rails' rich text capabilities.
3. Use one of the possible CSS libraries to style a Rails application.
4. Extend the React example to include create, update, and delete operations for CRUD.
5. Extend the Electron native example to include more than the CPU brand.
6. Create a form to use Rails' `has_many through` or `has_and_belongs_to_many` relationships. There are at least two approaches to this.
    a. Use `collection_check_boxes` on both sides of the relationship.
    b. Create a scaffold for the junction table with `collection_select` for each side of the relationship.

CHAPTER 5

Controllers

"Freedom is the only worthy goal in life. It is won by disregarding things that lie beyond our control"

Epictetus

Introduction to the Chapter

Controllers are where we spend a lot of our time. They are where the business logic (the behavior) of our applications resides and so they make each application unique. In general, controllers have a number of methods for the different operations needed for the models, and those methods also typically render a view once they're done.

Learning Outcomes

By the end of this chapter, you'll be able to do the following:

1. Create routes (URLs and verbs) appropriate to your applications, making them easier to navigate for both humans and other applications.
2. Use filters to screen how requests are preprocessed and create associated responses.
3. Generate methods that return files and dynamically create output from requests.
4. Generate useful integration (controller) and system tests that enable both regression and acceptance testing. These also facilitate effective refactoring, an important aspect of all our development.
5. Deploy your application to a publicly visible web server.

Key Terms

The following important **terms** will be introduced in this chapter.

- **Routing**
- **Verification and validation**
- **Inversion of Control**
- **Filters**
- **Cookies**
- **Integration and system testing**

Routing

Part of the Rails pipeline is **routing** (mapping) URLs and HTTP verbs to controller methods. Here's an example of a `rails routes` command that displays the current routes in a simple todo application.

Concept Leads to Code

```
     Prefix Verb   URI Pattern                  Controller#Action
      items GET    /items(.:format)             items#index
            POST   /items(.:format)             items#create
   new_item GET    /items/new(.:format)         items#new
  edit_item GET    /items/:id/edit(.:format)    items#edit
       item GET    /items/:id(.:format)         items#show
            PATCH  /items/:id(.:format)         items#update
            PUT    /items/:id(.:format)         items#update
            DELETE /items/:id(.:format)         items#destroy
```

You can also find this information when your server is running in development mode by going to `http://localhost:3000/rails/info/routes`. As an aside, you can also get the properties of the running development server by going to `http://localhost:3000/rails/info/properties`. The `Prefix` can (for example) be used in `_url` and `_path` in link and button helpers. The `Verb` is the HTTP verb and the `URI Pattern` matches the request from the browser. There are several interesting things to note in the `URI Pattern`. First, it is a pattern, where if a word starts with a colon, whatever matches at that place in the request is placed into a variable and is passed to the controller. The `.:format` allows a browser or another application to request `http://localhost:3000/items` and receive HTML, and `http://localhost:3000/items.json` and receive JSON. Those patterns that include the `:id` will pass the match into the controller as part of the `params` hash identified as `:id`. For example, `http://localhost:3000/items/17` will call the `show` method of the items controller with `params[:id] = 17`. This allows the `edit`, `show`, `update`, and `destroy` methods to be called with a specific item. The final column, labeled `Controller#Action` tells us which controller (in `app/controllers`) will be sent the message, and which method (`Action`) in that controller will receive the message.

The above eight routes are configured with a single line in the `config/routes.rb` file: `resources :items`. Routing in Rails is extraordinarily flexible, and as your applications become more complicated it's well worth your time to become versed in the flexibility.

Actions/Methods

In a controller, there are a number of methods that accept data from the router and perform operations on those data, and possibly the model (database). The first route returns all the items; there is one line in the `app/controller/items_controller` index method: `@items = Item.all`. It is important to know that the default behavior once a controller method is complete is to automatically search for a view in app/views/controller (app/views/items in this case) with the same name as the controller method (app/views/items/index.html.erb in this case). That file creates the appropriate HTML to list the items, typically using a loop on the @items passed in and calling an _item partial for each item. It is also important to understand that locals from a controller are automatically passed to the associated views so that @items is available in the associated views.

Filters

Rails provides the ability to call methods before, after, and around controller methods called **filters**. These are used for many different purposes, but let's initially see their use in the controllers created by a generator. Looking in app/controllers/items_controller.rb, we see a line before_action :set_item, only: %i[show edit update destroy]. This specifies that a set_item method will be called before calling show, edit, update, and destroy. As we can see from the routes above, these are the four methods that take specific item identifiers. There are two methods in scaffold-generated controllers at the bottom, one of them is set_modelname, and the other is modelname_params.

Concept Leads to Code

```
private
  # Use callbacks to share common setup or constraints between actions.
  def set_item
    @item = Item.find(params[:id])
  end

  # Only allow a list of trusted parameters through.
  def item_params
    params.require(:item).permit(:what, :when)
  end
```

For both show and edit, this is all that needs to be done in the controller as the default is to then call the associated view. Indeed, there don't have to be show and edit methods in the controller at all to get the proper functionality as the set_item and default view can do all the work; the scaffold generator puts empty methods in the controller as place holders should you want to add functionality to those.

The new method creates a via object via @item = Item.new and renders the app/views/items/new.html.erb file, that then renders the app/views/items/_form.html.erb file that creates the HTML for a form to enter the data and then submit via a POST to /items and as we can see from the route, those data are sent to the create method. In the create method, we see @item = Item.new(item_params) that calls Item.new with the results of the item_params method call. As we see above the method item_params is called to check that the proper parameters are allowed from the form submission. The params hash is automatically passed to the controller, but we need to make sure that only those values we want are allowed. As people are not required to use the forms we create or can add additional information on form submission (a type of injection attack that Rails calls mass assignment), we must limit the values to only those we want. The `require` and `permit` methods do just that: require that some fields be present and permit others to be used. There will be more fields in the model that we don't want users of our application access to, e.g. `created_at` is automatically created for us by Rails and we probably don't want a form submission to modify that. One of the times we must modify the `permit` is when we have a form for a `has_many` relationship and we want to pass in an array, such as from a `collection_check_boxes` field.

As we saw in the chapter on views, the JBuilder gem creates JSON output instead of HTML. The controllers must have code in them to help with this process. Let's look at the create method.

Concept Leads to Code

```
def create
  @item = Item.new(item_params)

  respond_to do |format|
    if @item.save
      format.html { redirect_to item_url(@item), notice: "Item was successfully
created." }
      format.json { render :show, status: :created, location: @item }
    else
      format.html { render :new, status: :unprocessable_entity }
      format.json { render json: @item.errors, status: :unprocessable_entity }
    end
  end
end
```

Here we see that the method can respond for either a successful or unsuccessful save, and for each either in HTML or JSON. For a successful save in HTML, the user is redirected to the newly created item with a message stating the item was successfully created. For JSON, the `show.json.jbuilder` template is called and the HTTP return value is set to 201, which denotes the successful creation of a resource. There are currently 59 different numeric codes that Rails can return. If the item wasn't saved, in HTML the `app/views/items/new.html.erb` template will be rendered with an HTML error code of 422 (unprocessable_entity). For JSON, a similar JSON error message will be returned.

The `render` method is a special one in Rails. It can only be called once in a controller method, and if you call it more than once you will receive a double render error. In the above create method, there is essentially a nested if as either `format.html or format.json` will match, but not both.

Request and Response Objects

Rails gives us access to exactly how a request was made via a request object. It contains a wealth of information such as the following.

1. The hostname and domain the request was sent to.
2. The HTTP verb used.

3. A hash of all the headers.
4. The port on the local machine the request arrived at.
5. The remote machine's IP address.

For the response object, here are some of the fields available.

1. body that contains the string to be returned.
2. The status code that is being returned.
3. The MIME content type of the response.

These two objects allow great flexibility of communication when you need it.

Members and Collections

Rails routing allows us to add RESTful routes in addition to the ones made by the `resources` directive in `config/routes.rb`. `member` adds a *RESTful* path that returns a single resource, `collection` adds a route that has multiple resources. For example, let's say we want to return the time created for a specific item so we can know how long ago it was created. This, in general, isn't displayed but we have the datum as Rails records it for us. We can create a `created_at` route to retrieve this information from an individual item by creating the route in `config/routes.rb` and a few modifications to the controller and views.

Concept Leads to Code

```
# config/routes.rb
  resources :items do
    member do
      get 'created_at'
    end
  end

# app/controllers/items_controller.rb
  def created_at
    @item.created_at
  end

# app/views/items/created_at.html.erb
<div id="<%= dom_id @item %>">
  <p>
    <strong>When:</strong>
    <%= @item.when %>
  </p>
</div>

# app/views/items/created_at.json.jbuilder
json.extract! @item, :when
json.url created_at_item_url(@item, format: :json)
```

If we instead want to search on one or more of the fields for an item, we have a couple of choices. The first is to pass the search string into the index method and display only those entries that match. This requires relatively few modifications to our existing application.

Concept Leads to Code

```
# app/views/items/index.html.erb
<p style="color: green"><%= notice %></p>

<h1>Items</h1>

<div id="items">
  <% @items.each do |item| %>
    <%= render item %>
    <p>
      <%= link_to "Show this item", item %>
    </p>
  <% end %>
</div>

<%= form_with url: items_url, method: :get do |form| %>
    <%= form.label :what_query, "Search for what:" %>
    <%= form.text_field :what_query %>
    <%= form.submit "Search" %>
<% end %>

<%= form_with url: items_url, method: :get do |form| %>
    <%= form.label :when_query, "Search for when:" %>
    <%= form.date_field :when_query %>
    <%= form.submit "Search" %>
<% end %>

<%= link_to "New item", new_item_path %>

# app/controllers/items_controller.rb
  def index
    if params[:what_query]
      @items = Item.where("what like ?", "%#{params[:what_query]}%")
    elsif params[:when_query]
      @items = Item.where('"when" like ?', "#{params[:when_query]}")
    else
      @items = Item.all
    end
  end
```

Here we're limiting the number of items returned from the `index` method using a `where` model method on `Item` records in the controller and reusing the rendering from the default `index` method. Note that if called with a `.json` suffix, the correct JSON is returned.

Another interesting possibility that the built-in Turbo (https://turbo.hotwired.dev/) methods allow for is autocomplete. The only thing that changes is the view. Let's say we have a movie application that has movie titles among other fields. We can make the type of index we have above and have a different search form. This search form references a Turbo frame found later in the page that wraps the HTML/ERB (`turbo_frame_tag "results"`) that displays the index and of course also the results of a search.

Concept Leads to Code

```
# app/controllers/movies_controller.rb
  def index
    @movies = if params[:query]
      Movie.where('title LIKE ?', "%#{params[:query]}%")
    else
      Movie.all
    end
  end

# app/views/movies/index.html.erb
<h1>Movies</h1>

<%= form_with(url: movies_path, method: :get,
  data: { turbo_frame: "results", turbo_action: "advance" }) do |form| %>
  Search
  <%= form.search_field(:query, value: params[:query],
    oninput: "this.form.requestSubmit()") %>
<% end %>

<%= turbo_frame_tag "results" do %>
  <div id="movies">
    <% @movies.each do |movie| %>
      <%= render movie %>
      <p>
        <%= link_to "Show this movie", movie %>
      </p>
    <% end %>
  </div>
<% end %>

<%= link_to "New movie", new_movie_path %>
```

A third possibility is having a separate method in the controller for searching. We need to set up a route to this method in `config/routes.rb`. As this method will return multiple results, a simple way to add this is a `collection` directive as shown below. It's important to use the get directive instead of the default `post` method in the form as searches are, in general, cacheable. Of course, if the data being searched changes often, caching may not be appropriate. The `search` method in the controller looks familiar; instead of creating a new `search.html.erb` file, we can reuse the `index.html.erb` by calling `render :index`.

Concept Leads to Code

```
# config/routes.rb
Rails.application.routes.draw do
  resources :movies do
    collection do
      get 'search'
    end
  end
end

# app/controllers/movies_controller.rb
  def search
    @movies = if params[:query]
      Movie.where('title LIKE ?', "%#{params[:query]}%")
    else
      Movie.all
    end
    render :index
  end

# app/views/movies/index.html.erb after the <h1>
<%= form_with url: search_movies_url, method: :get do |form| %>
    <%= form.text_field :query %>
    <%= form.submit "Search" %>
<% end %>
```

Streams

Rails controllers can also create streams of data to send to browsers. The `send_file` method specifies a file on the local server to send, typically being saved by the browser. You can override this default by specifying `disposition: inline` to the method. A very simple example could look like a single route in `config/routes.rb` and a single associated method in a controller.

Concept Leads to Code

```
# config/routes.rb
Rails.application.routes.draw do
  get '/toby', to: 'kitties#toby'
end

# app/controllers/kitties_controller.rb
class KittiesController < ApplicationController
  def toby
    send_file 'public/toby.png', disposition: 'inline'
  end
end
```

Rails also has a `send_data` method for dynamically generated content.

Cookies

Cookies are another way clients and servers communicate. They are sent via two HTTP headers: `Set-Cookie:` from the server, and `Cookie:` as a response from the browser. Cookies are a way of maintaining the state between a client and server as HTTP itself is a stateless protocol. We need to have some way for the server to recognize the client for functionality such as authenticated sessions, shopping carts, etc. Each of these requires more context than a single request/response cycle can provide, so the state is kept between the client and server via cookies. In Rails, at least a `session_id` and a `_csrf_token` are generated each time a client initially contacts a server. Note that the `session_id` isn't an authenticated session, you must use additional gems as described in the Security chapter. The `_csrf_token` is used to counteract Cross-Site Request Forgeries, also see the Security chapter. Here is an example of a cookie sent from a simple application.

Concept Leads to Code

```
Set-Cookie:
_todos_session=e8d4SOmNkXx6xml2Jp%2BLI2wROYHmCalBCsbY16ddvgmLyoWmtiM55VwQUIyPkb%2
BNpH6GPxQmk83hK%2FsFVhgfuJoZBjHUFW23wIvaij%2BxidUuSsdAvS53KqUdpZE7%2BOoOJKJsNfYIT
oc07%2BX7cdYOjKs3w1YCUEYNolJi%2B5vku3Wr0repWWDjDoginmHcYc9um9QCO9oCWVuTqkcFSbs1IK
e%2Bm%2FH%2BBmFezm3YQnE%2FLGqebNyi6%2FduKE86vC9U50dp2m%2FbPuNwkh81pl%2BmgmzBL%2Fr
7F3xExLCnelIRc%2FIBW8u0P586V%2BJqz%2BccuWpeWzXID9WKOOaTME1ZSoSQSMupfzULoo5xNZ%2Fg
dnI38IyBvmx02%2FaLrxZGZch9eYBTnSBBeLtifP6sdKboXZtT5Tpd9W%2B1WZZkYKoFRc88yafHkhJQG
iGiZzCTTpDVREjp6anASz4R2oAnzXIreM1bfbC8sH0ZQ1va527c4trodcbG--8xyBP5ALdEOQwFeJ--
muAY4yK4VbkNWp%2FzvfCiAA%3D%3D; path=/; HttpOnly; SameSite=Lax
```

The `_todos_session` is a long, randomly generated (not easily guessable) token that keeps track of the client/server state. We in general don't need to use this value directly as Rails keeps track of it for us. The path denotes where the cookie is valid for; here for any requests to the site but a cookie might be limited for use within a subdomain instead of an entire site. This cookie also specifies it should only be used for HTTP communication; other communication techniques such as FTP cannot be used. Finally, the `SameSite` specifies when the cookie will be sent from the client to the server. `Lax` means that it will always be sent when moving from one page to another on the same site. It also means that it will not be sent on a request to a different site but will be sent when following a link from a different site back to this site. This is the default behavior. There is also `Strict` that disallows the sending of the cookie when coming from a foreign site.

There are several cookie expiration timeout parameters; without any specification, the cookie expires when the window or browser closes. These are called session cookies. Some sites have a "Remember this browser" check box that creates a session using a cookie that spans multiple browser invocations, i.e.: contains an expiry date for some time into the future.

Another important value is the `Secure` cookie. This specifies that all cookie communication must happen via HTTPS, critical for production websites. Creating an HTTPS Rail server will be covered in the security chapter.

When your application needs to keep session data for a user, you can create cookies simply by adding to the `session` hash. You can retrieve all the values using the usual `session.each do |key, value|` hash loop.

The Flash

Another way to communicate between a controller and a view is the flash. This is a hash of values that lasts only for a single response. It is not passed as a cookie but is available in ERB files and is typically used for notifications. By default, there are two: `notice` and `alert`, though you can add more if you want. You might have already noticed their use in responding to a create or update via format.html `{ redirect_to todo_url(@todo), notice: "Todo was successfully created." }`. You can create notices and alerts directly in a controller via `flash[:notice] = "your string"` and `flash[:alert] = "your string"`. There are also convenience methods that allow you to use `flash.notice = "your string"` and `flash.alert = "your string"`. When a scaffold is created, Rails puts flash notices in the `index.html.erb` and `show.html.erb` files. If you want them to show up in all views, you can modify the `app/views/layouts/application.html.erb` file. Indeed, that is the file that contains the overall layout of the application so changes in that file are reflected on all pages, keeping things DRY.

Testing

Controller Tests

When a scaffold is created, many tests are created for the associated controller. Indeed, the only method not initially covered by the tests is show, but that's a relatively easy test to make due to its basic functionality.

Concept Leads to Code

```
test "should show one" do
  get todo_url(@todo.id)
  assert_response :success
end
```

When you add functionality to your controller, it's crucial to write tests for each part of the new functionality. The best case is that you write the tests before you write the code in keeping with test-driven development. Even if you write them after some amount of implementation, it's important to have regression tests and to document to expected behavior of your methods.

A test database is automatically created by Rails during **`rails test`**. The data in that database comes from the files in the `test/fixtures` directory, not from the usual `db` directory. The files in the `test/fixtures` directory are *YAML* (originally *Yet Another Markup Language*, now *YAML Ain't Markup Language*) files. The syntax of YAML files is relatively straightforward and YAML is used for data serialization. That is, it is used to describe a binary object or data structure as plain text. Non-tab indentation denotes the structure or nesting of data inside an object. Comments start with a # and continue to the end of the line. List items start with a -. Strings can be unquoted or quoted with double or single quotes. For a simple todo list, the `test/fixtures/todos.yml` file might look like the following.

Concept Leads to Code

```
one:
  item: MyString
  due: 2022-07-28

two:
  item: MyString
  due: 2022-07-28
```

This creates two todo's in the test database so that the controller tests have data to work with. Note that the string is the same in both; if you specified uniqueness in the model, you'll have to change one. The date defaults to the date the YAML file was created.

System Tests

Rails also creates end-to-end tests for scaffolds. You run these via **`rails test:system`**. These create a running instance of a browser and fill out and click on submit for forms, click on links, etc.; pretty much whatever a human can do on a web page. Rails uses Capybara (http://teamcapybara.github.io/capybara/) and Selenium (https://www.selenium.dev/) as defaults to automate interacting with a browser and examining the results. You'll see a browser (typically Chrome) while the tests are being run. You can also run the system test without bringing up a browser, making the tests faster, by changing a line in `test/application_system_test_case.rb` to read **`driven_by :selenium, using: :headless_chrome, screen_size: [1400, 1400]`**.

System tests can be very useful for the **verification** and **validation** of your application, and these can lead to using the system tests as acceptance tests. The difference between the two is sometimes expressed that validation asks, "Are you building the right thing?", and verification asks "Are you building it correctly?". That is, verification checks if the application meets the user specifications and validation checks if the users are willing to use the application. You might create an application that perfectly meets user specifications, but the users didn't know what they wanted, or the user environment has changed such that the application is no longer relevant, i.e.: is no longer a valid solution.

Deployment

Of course, once we develop an application, we need others to use it. There are many ways to deploy applications including the following.

- Pushing to servers using a file archive such as Java ARchive (JAR), Enterprise Application aRchive (EAR), or WAR (Web Application Resource) file that a server starts serving.
- Using a CI/CD pipeline to deploy the latest version of a branch.
- Using a Docker image to push to a server, especially to a Kubernetes (https://kubernetes.io/) cluster that can provision and load balance between many instances.

There are sites where we can experiment with deployment such as Heroku (https://devcenter.heroku.com/articles/getting-started-with-rails7) for very little cost. Heroku expects a Postgres database, so our `config/database.yml` needs to follow the example given as follows.

Concept Leads to Code

```
default: &default
  adapter: postgresql
  encoding: unicode
  pool: <%= ENV.fetch("RAILS_MAX_THREADS") { 5 } %>

development:
  <<: *default
  database: myapp_development

test:
  <<: *default
  database: myapp_test

production:
  <<: *default
  database: myapp_production
  username: myapp
  password: <%= ENV['MYAPP_DATABASE_PASSWORD'] %>
```

Once we've set up our database environment, we can publish our local application to Heroku via the following commands.

Concept Leads to Code

```
# Use the Heroku credentials you created.
heroku login
bundle lock --add-platform x86_64-linux --add-platform ruby
# Create an app container on Heroku.
heroku apps:create
# Add Postgres.
heroku addons:create heroku-postgresql:mini
# List the current apps.
heroku apps
# Add the app we just created.
heroku git:remote -a the app name
# Push our app.
git push heroku main
# Migrate the Postgres database.
heroku run rake db:migrate
# Use the smallest possible container.
heroku ps:scale web=1
# Make sure the instance is running.
heroku ps
# Open the app in our local browser.
heroku open
# Once we're done, remove everything so that we're not charged for
# resources we don't use.
heroku apps:destroy
```

Summary

Controllers differentiate behavior between applications. They interact with both the model and the view. They play a central role in how one web application is different from another and therefore is where application developers spend a lot of their effort. The methods in the controllers are called via the routes in the application and they interact with the model to persist the appropriate data and display the results of their work in a view. Creating tests for each method in a controller, and the application overall helps ensure that the application does what is specified (verification) and does what is desired or useful (validation).

Exercises

Directions: Use what you learned in this chapter to successfully complete the following tasks and exercises.

1. Create the necessary routes and methods required to expose the `updated_at` field in a data item.
2. Generate a thorough system test, including the expected HTML and CSS, for a page in an application using Selenium.
3. Craft a page that returns the contents of a file, typically from the `public` directory.
4. Add a search capability to an existing application.
5. Deploy your application to a remote publicly available server.

CHAPTER 6

Security

"If you know the enemy and know yourself, you need not fear the result of a hundred battles. If you know yourself but not the enemy, for every victory gained you will also suffer a defeat. If you know neither the enemy nor yourself, you will succumb in every battle."

Sun Tzu, The Art of War

Introduction

It is difficult to keep up with the number of security vulnerabilities that affect applications. In 2022, the CVE database (https://www.cve.org/) published an average of 70 new vulnerabilities or exposures a day. Not all of these are from web applications of course, but a quick search shows that through the years 15,149 are from SQL vulnerabilities and 21,758 are from cross-site scripting. As more and more devices, including Internet of Things (IoT) devices, have built-in web servers, the attack surface increases, as does our responsibility to be cognizant of security concerns in the applications we build.

Learning Outcomes

By the end of this chapter, you'll be able to do the following.

1. Create more secure applications that are resistant to SQL and XSS injections.
2. Generate applications that require authentication and authorization.
3. Construct applications whose data are encrypted both at rest and in flight.
4. Augment your server with cross-origin resource-sharing directives.
5. Browse the dark web.

Key Terms

The following important **terms** will be introduced in this chapter.

- **Authentication**
- **Authorization**
- **Encryption at rest and in transit**
- **Static and dynamic code analysis**
- **Injections**
- **The dark web**

Active Record Encryption

Rails allows us to encrypt fields in databases controlled by active record. As much of the data we store is sensitive, we want to encrypt those data we have so that when they are exfiltrated they cannot be read. There are two general types of **encryption** in Rails.

1. *Non-deterministic.* In this case, given the same text more than once, Rails will produce different encrypted text. This is a stronger way of encryption but does not allow for searching for a value in a field. This is completely appropriate for fields such as passwords, but much less so for items we do want to search on such as book titles, etc.
2. *Deterministic.* Here, when given the same text multiple times, Rails will return the same encrypted version, allowing us to perform searches on those data.

We need to first create the credentials that will be used to encrypt the data. This is done by running **`bin/rails db:encryption:init`**. This command has output similar to the following, but do not use these specific lines in your application as others might be able to decrypt your data when exfiltrated.

Concept Leads to Code

```
Add this entry to the credentials of the target environment:

active_record_encryption:
  primary_key: a77fQ01BeMehQtOaDy0m0vWVTLRBvInQ
  deterministic_key: cXf5O9hIpZuySQDuAxY4H8pk6aL3aduk
  key_derivation_salt: LbZooLJhrUCdqWliVxlwgcqmOtPsQnRN
```

You will then need to use **`bin/rails credentials:edit`** and add those four lines to the credentials. Now we are ready to encrypt fields in models. For example, in our usual Todo application, we can encrypt the what to do field by putting in a single line in **`app/models/item.rb`** that states **`encrypts :what`** to encrypt what we need to do. If we want to be able to search on the what, we instead need **`encrypts :what, deterministic: true`**. Either way, we now see encrypted data in the database. Here's what one entry looks like.

Concept Leads to Code

```
INSERT INTO items
VALUES(1,'{"p":"pe8n","h":{"iv":"yFiXHOKTlDoMTszy","at":"1HVSccg9M2qzSla/
sdD+lQ=="}}','2023-04-19','2023-04-19 10:46:30.880533','2023-04-19
10:46:30.880533');
```

Another issue we must deal with is testing assumes that data from the YAML test fixture files are entered into the test database unencrypted. This breaks many of our tests. We need to put the line `config.active_record.encryption.encrypt_fixtures = true` into the `config/environments/test.rb` file to make our tests work again.

Authentication

There are two related concepts whose words are similar, but it is important to differentiate between the two. They are **authentication** and **authorization** (often abbreviated *auth/n* and *auth/z*). Authentication is proving who you are. There are several approaches to authenticating who you are; these are typically called factors. The top three are as follows.

1. Something you know. These are passwords, PINs, etc.
2. Something you have. These are physical items such as passports, driver's licenses, a phone to receive text messages or that has an authentication application, etc.
3. Something you are. These are biometrics: fingerprint or facial recognition, etc.

Multifactor Authentication (*MFA*, or sometimes two of these: *2FA*) uses more than one factor such as a password and a text message.

Rails has an excellent gem for authentication named Devise (https://github.com/heartcombo/devise). It can save credentials locally in a database or use Omniauth (https://github.com/omniauth/omniauth) for external authenticators. While it is more complicated to use an external authenticator, it will prevent you from saving any user credentials so when a breach occurs in your application, no credentials can be lost. Devise has many useful features.

1. If you have an emailer configured, Devise will send confirmation and password recovery emails to users.
2. It will track logins, including failed attempts and timestamps. You can configure how many failed attempts will lock an account and how accounts can be unlocked, either via email or a certain amount of time passing.
3. You can configure session timeout so that if a user is inactive for a certain amount of time, they must re-authenticate.

To install Devise for an application, use the following steps.

Concept Leads to Code

```
bundle add devise
rails generate devise:install
rails generate devise User
```

Certain Devise features must be enabled in **app/models/user.rb** and in **db/migrate/[…]_devise_create_users.rb** before db:migrate is run. How the additional features are configured is specified in the **config/initializers/devise.rb** file.

You must have a default route in **config/routes.rb** such as root **"items#index"**. In the controllers where you want authenticated users, put a **before_action :authenticate_user!** at the top of the file. You should also want to add a logout link in the appropriate HTML files that looks like **<%= link_to "Log out", destroy_user_session_path, data: { "turbo-method": :delete } %>**.

Devise has some test helpers so that our **integration** tests can run without worrying about managing an authenticated session. The top of a controller test needs two lines inserted.

Concept Leads to Code

```
class ItemsControllerTest < ActionDispatch::IntegrationTest
  include Devise::Test::IntegrationHelpers

  setup do
    sign_in users(:one)
    @item = items(:one)
  end
```

The **test/fixtures/users.yml** file should also be edited so that there is a single user placed in the test database, it can be as simple as **foo: {}**.

Authorization

Authorization is a complicated topic with many different approaches. A popular gem for Rails is CanCanCan (https://github.com/CanCanCommunity/cancancan). CanCanCan uses an ability-based approach that decouples users from what they can perform in an application. Decisions on authorizations can be made on many more factors other than how someone logged in. That said, the simplest initial approach is checking for login status, and CanCanCan integrates well with Devise. Assuming you are already using Devise, you'll need to do a **bundle install cancancan** and a **rails generate cancan:ability**. This creates an **app/models/ability.rb** file where a wide variety of abilities and permissions can be defined. Here's a very simple example.

Concept Leads to Code

```
# frozen_string_literal: true

class Ability
  include CanCan::Ability

  def initialize(user)
    return unless user.present?
      can :read, :all
  end
end
```

This only checks that someone is logged in before allowing them to read a resource. For a posts resource, we can edit **app/controllers/posts_controller.rb** to add both the Devise and CanCanCan directives at the top.

Concept Leads to Code

```
class PostsController < ApplicationController
  before_action :authenticate_user!
  before_action :set_post, only: %i[ show edit update destroy ]
  load_and_authorize_resource
```

Again, this is a simplistic approach to authorization and CanCanCan allows a great deal more flexibility.

HTTPS

All the applications we've built so far have used HTTP as the transmission protocol and of course we never want to do this for a live application. We must use *HTTPS* to keep all data secure during transmission. It is relatively straightforward to do so, though we first need a public/private key pair to pass to the server. We can generate a self-signed certificate using OpenSSL (https://www.openssl.org/). Once installed you can create the two necessary files via **openssl req -x509 -sha256 -nodes -newkey rsa:2048 -days 365 -keyout localhost.key -out localhost.crt**. The `.key` file is the private key and must not be readable except by the server or all communication will be compromised. Do not, for example, check that file into a public repository. The `.crt` is the *self-signed certificate* file that we can trust in our browser during development. You will need to answer the following questions to create the self-signed certificate. In general, you don't need to tell the truth as we're going to end up instructing our local browser to accept the certificate.

Concept Leads to Code

```
Country Name (2 letter code) []:
State or Province Name (full name) []:
Locality Name (eg, city) []:
Organization Name (eg, company) []:
Organizational Unit Name (eg, section) []:
Common Name (eg, fully qualified host name) []:
Email Address []:
```

Once we have these two files, we can start the web server via **`rails s -b 'ssl://localhost:3000?key=localhost.key&cert=localhost.crt'`**. The `-b` argument tells the Rails server to bind (attach) to a specific port; it also understands how to process the key and certificate files. We can now surf to https://localhost:3000/ but we'll get an error message similar to the following.

Concept Leads to Code

```
Your connection is not private
Attackers might be trying to steal your information from localhost (for example,
passwords, messages, or credit cards). Learn more
NET::ERR_CERT_AUTHORITY_INVALID
```

This is saying that your browser does not trust the issuer of the certificate as in general it shouldn't. It should only trust certificates validated by *certificate authorities (CA)*. Browsers come with a list of trusted CAs. While the certificate isn't valid, the connection is now encrypted using, in this case, TLS_AES_256_GCM_SHA384, 256-bit keys, and TLS1.3. To connect to your local server, you'll need to click on the Advanced button of the browser warning page and allow the browser to complete the connection.

For production purposes, you'll need to have a certificate signed by a CA. Each different server or deployment site has different approaches to specifying where the associated files are placed. The Let's Encrypt (https://letsencrypt.org/) organization will provide you with free, trusted, certificates so there is no reason to ever deploy unencrypted applications.

Browser Security

While we're mostly concerned about server security in this book, browser security does play a role. Specifically, we need to make sure that when we use a non-Rails frontend to access the JSON API, we need to make minor modifications to our server to allow this.

Same-Origin Policy

In general, browsers trust the content of sites they explicitly visit, whether the user enters the URL or follows a link. Browsers trust users to do the right thing. Once at a site, another question becomes:

which resources should a browser trust that are referenced by that site? A simple answer is to allow the reading resources from the same origin using the Same-Origin Policy (SOP). Here, the origin is the combination of the HTTP scheme, host, and port number. Consider `http://www.example.com/pathA`. This matches `http://www.example.com/pathB` but not `https://www.example.com/pathA`, `http://host.example.com/pathA`, nor `http://www.example.com:3000/pathA`. The SOP does allow for a few exceptions; examples include the following.

1. The reading of scripts using `<script>src=…</script>` elements.
2. Similarly, the reading of CSS using `<link rel="stylesheet" …>` elements.
3. Media elements such as `<img>`, `<video>`, and `<audio>`.
4. Form submission (`POST`) to another site as SOP is concerned with the reading of malicious resources, not the writing.

While allowing these carries a certain amount of risk, their use is so pervasive (and their content is often hosted in CDNs) that not allowing them would break much of the web. What the SOP doesn't allow is scripts running from a different origin.

The SOP can lead to API calls being blocked by the browser. If, for example, the browser loads a SPA from localhost at port 3001 and that SPA requests data from localhost port 3000, the content from port 3000 won't be allowed by the browser and the following error will appear in the browser console.

Concept Leads to Code

```
Cross-Origin Request Blocked: The Same Origin Policy disallows reading the
remote resource at http://localhost:3000/items.json. (Reason: CORS header
'Access-Control-Allow-Origin' missing). Status code: 200.
```

Note again, SOP is a browser, not a server restriction. There are browser extensions that relax the SOP; these are in general not recommended as they open up security issues and will only work for the browser in which they are installed, all other browsers will continue to receive the same error. A better approach is to have servers state what origins they trust and ask browsers to trust them too via CORS.

Cross-Origin Resource Sharing

Cross-Origin Resource Sharing (CORS) is an HTTP header-based approach to sharing those resources that a server trusts with a client/browser. For Rails, there is a gem for that: Rack CORS (https://github.com/cyu/rack-cors). This gem allows you to specify what resources you trust that don't come directly from your site; that is those that would violate the SOP constraints. In the example above, if a script is served from a different site and wants to access resources from our application, the browser will block the request. To send the appropriate headers, we first must do a **`bundle install rack-cors`** and then create a configuration in **`config/initializers/cors.rb`**. A generic configuration could look like the following.

Concept Leads to Code

`Rails.application.config.middleware.insert_before 0, Rack::Cors do`

```
Rails.application.config.middleware.insert_before 0, Rack::Cors do
  allow do
    origins "localhost:3001"

    resource "*",
      headers: :any,
      methods: [:get, :post, :put, :patch, :delete, :options, :head]
  end
end
```

It's best not to wildcard the `origins` directive with a `*` as that would allow scripts from anywhere to request resources. You can certainly tighten access to specific resources and methods as appropriate. Here is a request and response, with many headers elided, based on the CORS file above.

Concept Leads to Code

```
# request
GET /items.json HTTP/1.1
Host: localhost:3000
Referer: http://localhost:3001/
Origin: http://localhost:3001

# response
HTTP/1.1 200 OK
access-control-allow-origin: http://localhost:3001
access-control-allow-methods: GET, POST, PUT, PATCH, DELETE, OPTIONS, HEAD
```

Another approach is to place the scripts you want to allow in the `public` or `app/javascript` directory, so they don't cross origins and cause the associated browser errors.

Injections

An **injection** compromise against a web application uses specially crafted input to expose data or trick users into entering personal information. There are several different types of injection attacks.

SQL

These injections are called *SQL injections (SQLi)*, though they can be used against a wide variety of databases, not just SQL databases. A simple type of these is used against queries that a user is allowed to submit but expands the scope of the query far beyond what is intended. For example, an application might allow a user to search for their information via an email address. A typical SQL query from a form would look like `SELECT * FROM person WHERE email='alice@example.com'`. The expectation is this would match a single record. However, SQL is a very flexible language and if we can spoof the name so it matches many records, we can exfiltrate a lot of useful data from a web application. SQL has the usual logical operations such as ANDs and ORs, and we can form tautologies (expressions that are always true) using them. Looking at the above query, if we can convert it to `SELECT * FROM person WHERE email='foo' OR '1' = '1'`, the OR statement will match all the records in the account table.

Say we have a form that has a search field such as `<%= form.search_field(:query, value: params[:query]) %>` that is sent to a controller with a naive query such as `Person.where("email LIKE '%#{params[:query]}%'")`. In general, we expect that a user would enter 'armando' and Rails would execute `SELECT "people".* FROM "people" WHERE (email LIKE '%armando%')`. Note the `%` is a wildcard in SQL. However, we can enter `foo' OR '%' = '` that converts the query into an SQL statement that looks like `SELECT "people".* FROM "people" WHERE (email LIKE '%foo' OR '%' = '%')`. Here, the `%` is being treated as a string, not a wildcard, and the OR statement forms a tautology. Now, all the people are returned as the OR tautology matches all the records. We have injected text into a form that compromised the security of the application.

In Rails, it is simple to disallow many types of SQLi injections by using the `?` placeholder in queries. The search for an email address above can be safely and easily rewritten as `Person.where("email LIKE ?", "%#{params[:query]}%")`. The `LIKE ?` invokes Rails' SQLi protection mechanisms and those remove the tautology injection. Even if you know a lot of SQL, it is worth taking the time to make sure you are using Rails' protections to their full extent.

Brakeman and Rubocop

It must be said that the two `.where` statements look a lot alike. One has a `?` and one doesn't. How can we make sure we're using the correct form? Happily, there is a static analysis tool called Brakeman that can help. In general, there are two types of program analysis tools.

1. **Static**. These analyze the program text when the application is not running. Static here means before the program is run and these tools look at the code we've written looking for typical errors we make.
2. **Dynamic**. These tools look at programs as they are being run, tracing the execution of the instructions.

Both types can find memory, performance, security, etc., concerns, though in general dynamic tools emphasize concerns such as memory misuse and performance as these are typically more visible as the application runs.

Brakeman is a static analysis tool created specifically for Rails applications. **`gem install brakeman`** installs it and we simply type **`brakeman`** in the application directory we want analyzed. For the specific injection error above, Brakeman reports the following.

Concept Leads to Code

```
== Warnings ==

Confidence: High
Category: SQL Injection
Check: SQL
Message: Possible SQL injection
Code: Person.where("email LIKE '%#{params[:query]}%'")
File: app/controllers/people_controller.rb
Line: 20
```

Another excellent static analysis tool is Rubocop (https://github.com/rubocop/rubocop-rails) and it can analyze a wide variety of Ruby and Rails concerns. We must analyze our applications for security flaws and include those analyses in our Continuous Integration/Continuous Deployment workflows. Web applications are ubiquitous and gather an incredible amount of *Personally Identifiable Information (PII)*; we are morally bound to protect those data to the best of our ability.

If you are interested in learning more about injections and other forms of web application compromise, please see https://www.zaproxy.org/ and https://owasp.org/www-project-webgoat/.

Cross-Site Scriping

Another type of injection is *Cross-Site Scripting (XSS)*. In this compromise, a bad actor injects a script into a text field. When another user displays the text, the script is inadvertently run in the user's browser. This works even if a user has authenticated as browsers trust content from sites the user directs them to either directly or by following a link; via the Same-Origin Policy (SOP). For example, if there is a comment field where users can enter any text they want, they can add `<script>alert("XSS!")</script>` as part of a comment. When someone else reads the comment, the script is run. This script isn't malicious of course, but there are many examples of malicious scripts. Keep in mind scripts in the browser can modify almost anything: all content on a page, the site history, and take a user to a completely different site.

Rails' has built-in protection against XSS attacks. Users can enter scripts into fields and while they will be persisted in the database, Rails escapes XSS scripts before displaying them. Note that we can subvert this protection, but of course, **do not do this**. One way is to use `<%==` in an ERB file instead of `<%=`. You can also use `html_safe` as in `<%= person.name.html_safe %>` or `raw` as in `<%= raw person.name %>`, but all of these leave your application vulnerable to XSS injections.

Cross-Site Request Forgery

A *Cross-Site Request Forgery (CSRF)* occurs when one web page sends a request to another website. This type of attack typically relies on a user being logged in to the target website. A simple, typically not dangerous type of cross-site scripting is known as a web bug. One approach to creating a web bug is to use HTML's `img` element to request a resource from another site using a GET. In the following example, the request does go to the Rails server, and the resource is returned, but no harm is done, except using the network, CPU, memory, etc. resources associated with fulfilling the request. Web bugs are invisible (unless you look at the page source) and are often used to track people from website to website to send them targeted advertisements.

Concept Leads to Code

```
<!DOCTYPE HTML>
<html>
  <head>
    <title>Web bug demo</title>
  </head>
  <body>
<img src="http://localhost:3000/people/1" width="0" height="0" border="0">
  </body>
</html>

# Rails console output
Started GET "/people/1" for ::1 at 2023-05-06 14:48:01 -0600
Processing by PeopleController#show as HTML
  Parameters: {"id"=>"1"}
  Person Load (0.9ms)  SELECT "people".* FROM "people" WHERE "people"."id" = ?
LIMIT ?  [["id", 1], ["LIMIT", 1]]
  ↳ app/controllers/people_controller.rb:69:in `set_person'
  Rendering layout layouts/application.html.erb
  Rendering people/show.html.erb within layouts/application
  Rendered people/_person.html.erb (Duration: 3.5ms | Allocations: 353)
  Rendered people/show.html.erb within layouts/application (Duration: 15.6ms |
Allocations: 1721)
  Rendered layout layouts/application.html.erb (Duration: 36.0ms | Allocations:
4824)
Completed 200 OK in 96ms (Views: 38.2ms | ActiveRecord: 4.5ms | Allocations:
25486)
```

Here, even though the user didn't request the image explicitly, the request is sent and all the usual information (IP address, etc.) is sent that can be used to uniquely identify a person.

A more nefarious approach is to send POSTs (or PUTs, PATCHs, or DELETEs) to the target website, typically via a script. Here's an example web page that does just that and the DELETE request is sent to the Rails server. In this instance, Rails' CSRF protection mechanism refuses to authenticate the request.

Concept Leads to Code

```
<!DOCTYPE HTML>
<html>
  <head>
    <title>CSRF</title>
  </head>
  <body onload="document.forms[0].submit()">
    <form action="http://localhost:3000/people/1" method="POST">
      <input type="hidden" name="_method" value="delete" autocomplete="off" />
    </form>
  </body>
</html>

# Rails console output
Started DELETE "/people/1" for ::1 at 2023-05-06 15:19:15 -0600
Processing by PeopleController#destroy as HTML
  Parameters: {"id"=>"1"}
Can't verify CSRF token authenticity.
Completed 422 Unprocessable Entity in 1ms (ActiveRecord: 0.0ms | Allocations:
236)
```

This didn't work against our server because Rails automatically adds a hidden value in the forms it creates and checks that it is returned on the form submission. The value changes each time a form is loaded. Other servers may well not check as closely. Here is what a Rails authenticity token looks like in a form: `<input type="hidden" name="authenticity_token" value="CaJ0OO…" autocomplete="off" />`.

In this way, Rails makes CSRF attacks much more difficult as the attack site can't in general know the target site's form `authenticity_token` and so can't send it with the nefarious request.

CSRFs are more dangerous the more sensitive a site is of course. Financial institutions use many techniques to reduce your exposure including these types of single-use tokens, encouraging you to log out when you're done using the site (this invalidates your session), and forcibly logging you out after you're inactive for some amount of time.

The Dark Web

No discussion of the web is complete without discussion of the **dark web**. There is the *surface web*: those parts of the web that are available to everyone and therefore indexed by search engines. There is the *deep web*: those parts of the web that require credentials to view such as school, financial, medical, etc., accounts. The usual assumption is the deep web has more content than the surface web. Then there is the dark web. This is easily accessed by downloading a special browser from https://www.torproject.org/download/. TOR stands for The Onion Router, an approach to sending information through multiple machines on the internet to anonymize communication. In this way, TOR is what we call an overlay network. Anyone can become part of the TOR network by downloading the server software at https://community.torproject.org/onion-services/setup/install/. In general, there are three types of nodes in a TOR connection.

1. Guard. These are where a browser initially connects to.
2. Middle. These anonymize the communication. In a specific circuit, there may be any number of middle nodes.
3. Exit. These are where the circuit exits to the regular web.

There is an initial list of guard nodes and directories in a TOR application. There is also a dynamic directory of guard, middle, and exit nodes available via TOR servers and a client can create an end-to-end circuit based on current data. These circuits typically change on an ongoing basis in clients; ten or so minutes is a typical time frame. The client can also create a new circuit at any time.

When a packet traverses the TOR network, it has several layers of routing information, each encrypted and invisible to the overall circuit. As the packet traverses the network, one layer of routing is decrypted and peeled off, giving rise to the term onion. Any node is aware of the previous and next nodes, but after two hops the initial location and final destinations cannot be derived from the packet. This very effectively anonymizes the communication.

All of this allows you to browse the surface or deep web anonymously, but that is not the typical use case for a TOR browser.

Hidden Services

TOR gives you the capability to create *hidden services*—pretty much any service available on the surface web including web, chat, and email servers. These are where much of the activity in the dark web occurs. While many organizations have servers in both the surface and dark web, much of the traffic that occurs in the dark web is for sites that would be illegal on the surface web. There have been many famous markets (The Silk Road, Alphabay, etc.) that have sold illicit drugs, credit cards, etc. It is simple to create a hidden service, only a few lines need to be changed to point the TOR network at a server running on your machine. Several things are interesting about the rise of the dark web.

1. It was created by the U.S. government, specifically the U.S. Naval Research Laboratory, and continues to be supported with government funds.
2. It was recognized that if all traffic through the TOR network was related to the U.S. government it would be an obvious target. It was then opened to anyone to decrease the signal-to-noise ratio (add more noise) and therefore decrease the possibility of capturing and decoding U.S. government communication.
3. TOR arrived before Bitcoin and other cryptocurrencies, but those cryptocurrencies greatly accelerated the use of the dark web. Now, someone could not only be anonymous, but they could also pay with anonymous currency allowing the dark web illicit markets to flourish.
4. Recently, some markets and cryptocurrency wallets have been infiltrated by law enforcement, leading to the arrest and imprisonment of those implicated. Also, when a hidden service is compromised, all the usual PII is available to law enforcement or the exfiltrators, just as with the surface web.

You can tell when you're accessing a hidden service as the address will end in `.onion`. Please exercise a great deal of caution when browsing the dark web. Again, most of the sites have illicit content—otherwise they'd be on the surface web. The sites can also contain web bugs as outlined above, placing illicit images, etc. in your browser's cache.

Summary

The need for secure applications has never been more evident. The breaches leading to ransomware and the exfiltration of intellectual property, personally identifiable information, medical records, etc. continue to increase. While web applications can't be blamed for every breach, there are relatively simple steps we can take when creating web applications that can help mitigate the damage done when a breach occurs. Encrypting data at rest and in flight is part of the solution. Making sure our applications aren't vulnerable to injection attacks, and proper authentication and authorization are others. In the end, all users of our applications trust that we have their best interests in mind and that we are being moral and ethical with the data they provide, so we must do all we can to not violate that trust.

Exercises

Directions: Use what you learned in this chapter to complete the following tasks and exercises.

1. Use active record encryption for one or more fields in your application. You'll need to decide which data should have deterministic or non-deterministic encryption.
2. Add authentication to an application using Devise.
3. Add authorization to an application using a combination of Devise and CanCanCan. You'll need to decide what resource operations should be allowed for which category of users.
4. Create a self-signed certificate and private key to serve encrypted network communication between your server and your local client.
5. The Open Worldwide Application Security Project® (https://owasp.org/) has many excellent resources to help building more secure web applications. Download WebGoat (https://owasp.org/www-project-webgoat/), probably the Docker image is easiest to install (currently https://hub.docker.com/r/webgoat/webgoat-8.0) and the Zed Attack Proxy (https://www.zaproxy.org/download/) and practice attacking a web application that is vulnerable on purpose. Injection attacks are particularly easy. Look at the code to see how the exploits are created.
6. Download the TOR browser and explore the dark web. Two sites to start with are The Hidden Wiki (http://zqktlwiuavvvqqt4ybvgvi7tyo4hjl5xgfuvpdf6otjiycgwqbym2qad.onion/wiki/index.php/Main_Page) and TorLinks (http://torlinksge6enmcyyuxjpjkoouw4oorgdgeo7ftnq3zodj7g2zxi3kyd.onion/). Be careful in where you go, the data you enter in any web site, and the content you view. You are legally liable for your actions on any web site, surface, deep, or dark.

APPENDIX A

Installation

"The environment is everything that isn't me."

Albert Einstein

Introduction

The first challenge we all face when creating an application is creating relevant and stable development/test/production environments. Indeed, most people's experience is that we spend an inordinate amount of time creating, aligning, upgrading, and maintaining our environments. Ruby and Rails are relatively easy to install, but there are always platform challenges. Containerization (here: Docker) can help with creating development, testing, and deployment environments. If you already have a working RoR 7 environment, you can safely skip this chapter.

Learning Outcomes

By the end of this chapter, you'll be able to do the following.

1. Install Ruby and Rails on your local machine and create a simple web application.
2. Use a containerized RoR development environment to create a simple web application.

Key Terms

The following important **terms** will be introduced in this chapter.

- **Development, testing, and deployment environments**
- **Installation on Linux, Windows, and OSX**

Windows

There are two major approaches to creating a RoR environment on Windows: use the *Windows Subsystem for Linux (WSL)* and use the **Linux** approach to Ruby and Rails or download a *Ruby installer.*

Windows Subsystem for Linux (WSL)

This method requires a version of **Windows** beyond the Home version, e.g.: Education or Pro should both work. First, install a Linux version using WSL. Bring up PowerShell and enter **`wsl -install`**. You can choose which Linux distribution to install; the default is Ubuntu. To see the list of available distributions, enter `wsl --list -online`. You can install multiple distributions if you want. Now bring up a terminal to use the Linux package manager to see if the correct version of Ruby is available. The following command **`apt search ruby`** will show the various (and typically plentiful!) packages related to Ruby. Here, we're looking for a version that starts with 3. If there isn't one directly available via the apt manager, we must use a different approach.

rbenv

There are several version managers for Ruby, this book recommends *rbenv* (https://github.com/rbenv/rbenv). rbenv is typically available via Linux package managers, so the following will install it on Debian/Ubuntu systems: **`sudo apt install rbenv`**. The `sudo` command allows you to elevate your permissions for the one command (to the "root" user) to write files to special places in the operating system. You should use `sudo` with great care as it can do a great deal of damage if used recklessly. You can then set up rbenv via the following.

Concept Leads to Code

```
rbenv init
# Load rbenv automatically by appending
# the following to ~/.bash_profile:

eval "$(rbenv init - bash)"
```

Do as it says and add that line at the end of your `~/.bash_profile` file so that rbenv works every time you log in. rbenv creates a directory in your home (~) directory named `.rbenv`. In there, there are two important directories: `shims` and `versions`. For rbenv to work, the `~/.rbenv/shims` directory must occur early in your `$PATH` environment variable. For example:

Concept Leads to Code

```
echo $PATH
/home/beaty/.rbenv/shims:/home/beaty/bin:/usr/local/sbin:/usr/local/bin:/usr/
sbin:/usr/bin:/sbin:/bin
```

shows that the shims directory is before other possible places a ruby executable might reside. To find the stable versions of Ruby, do:

Concept Leads to Code

```
rbenv install -l
2.6.9
2.7.5
3.0.3
3.1.1
jruby-9.3.4.0
mruby-3.0.0
rbx-5.0
truffleruby-22.0.0.2
truffleruby+graalvm-22.0.0.2
```

If you don't see many or any, you might need to update rbenv's plugin directory for ruby-build via

Concept Leads to Code

```
mkdir -p "$(rbenv root)"/plugins
git clone https://github.com/rbenv/ruby-build.git "$(rbenv root)"/plugins/ruby-
build
```

Now you should be able to install a Ruby version that starts with 3:

Concept Leads to Code

```
rbenv install 3.1.1
Downloading openssl-1.1.1n.tar.gz...
-> https://dqw8nmjcqpjn7.cloudfront.net/
40dceb51a4f6a5275bde0e6bf20ef4b91bfc32ed57c0552e2e8e15463372b17a
Installing openssl-1.1.1n...
Installed openssl-1.1.1n to /Users/stevebeaty/.rbenv/versions/3.1.1

Downloading ruby-3.1.1.tar.gz...
-> https://cache.ruby-lang.org/pub/ruby/3.1/ruby-3.1.1.tar.gz
Installing ruby-3.1.1...
ruby-build: using readline from homebrew
Installed ruby-3.1.1 to /Users/stevebeaty/.rbenv/versions/3.1.1
```

You can now check which Ruby you're running and the version number:

Concept Leads to Code

```
which ruby
/Users/stevebeaty/.rbenv/shims/ruby
ruby --version
ruby 3.1.1p18 (2022-02-18 revision 53f5fc4236) [x86_64-darwin20]
```

rbenv's real power is that we can have multiple versions of Ruby and Rails on a single machine. As we develop more applications using RoR, we'll have different versions of Ruby and Rails for each. Being able to easily switch to the version an application was developed with makes new development, enhancements, and bug fixes much easier.

Ruby Installer

Go to https://rubyinstaller.org/downloads/ and choose the recommended version with the devkit—as of this writing Ruby+Devkit 3.1.2-1 (x64). This will install everything you need for Ruby, and you can manage it as you do with other software packages you install. There are a number of screens that will come up during installation, though happily, the defaults are reasonable. Here's the first where you must accept the license after having read and understood it.

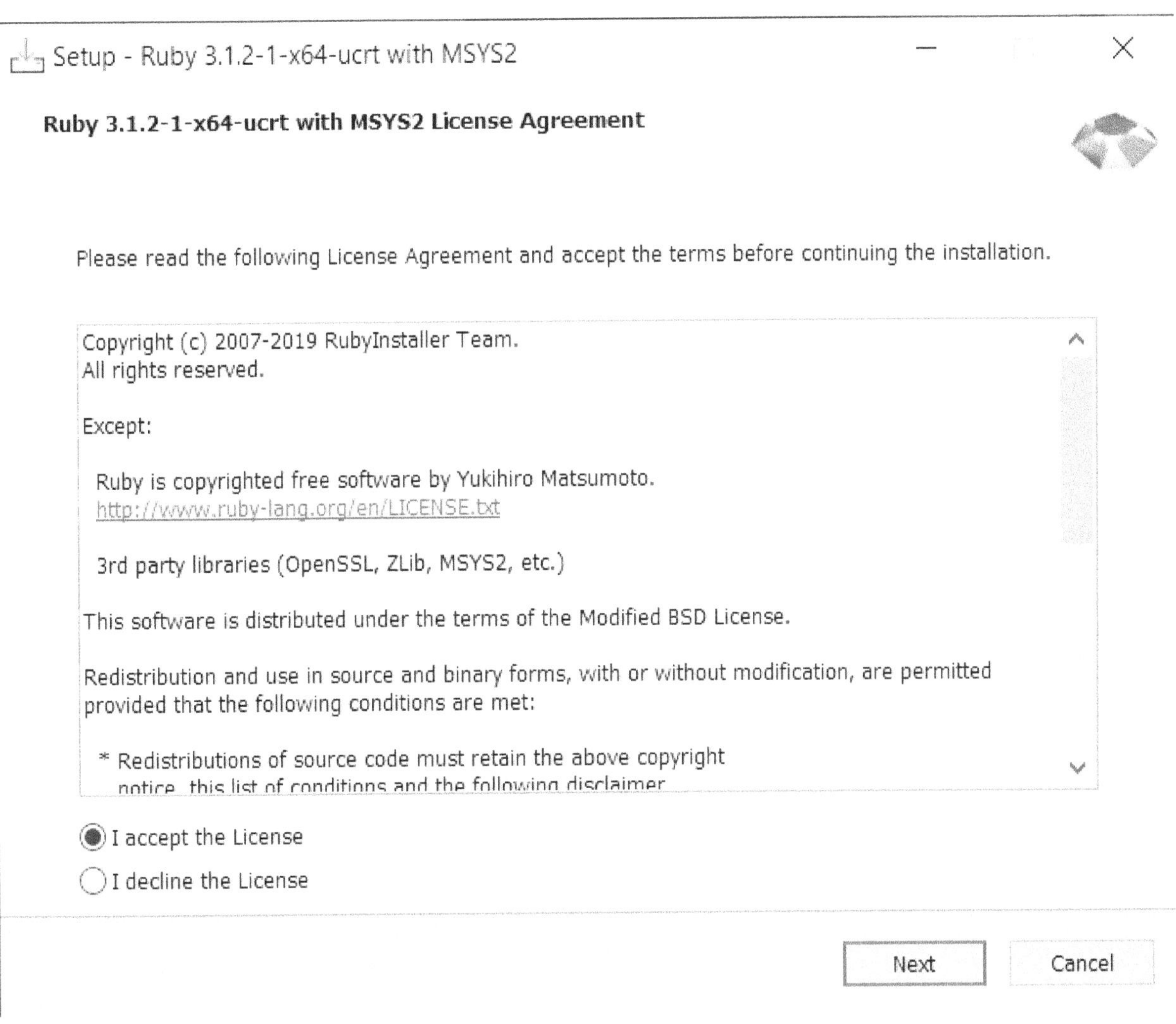

Copyright © by RubyInstaller.

The next asks what you want to install: the defaults (everything) are what you want.

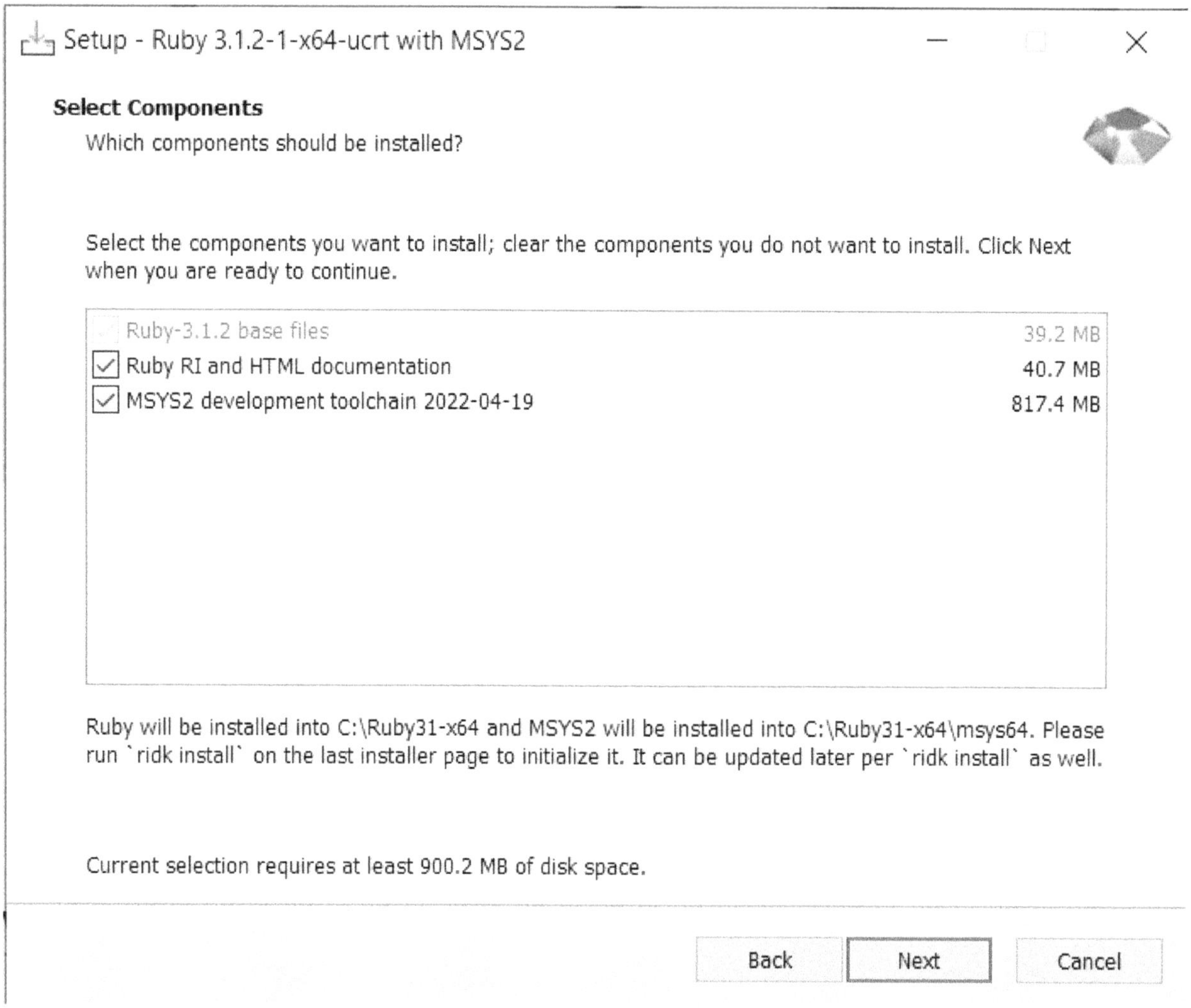

Setup - Ruby 3.1.2-1-x64-ucrt with MSYS2

Select Components

Which components should be installed?

Select the components you want to install; clear the components you do not want to install. Click Next when you are ready to continue.

Component	Size
Ruby-3.1.2 base files	39.2 MB
Ruby RI and HTML documentation	40.7 MB
MSYS2 development toolchain 2022-04-19	817.4 MB

Ruby will be installed into C:\Ruby31-x64 and MSYS2 will be installed into C:\Ruby31-x64\msys64. Please run `ridk install` on the last installer page to initialize it. It can be updated later per `ridk install` as well.

Current selection requires at least 900.2 MB of disk space.

Back Next Cancel

IMG A.2

After that, a screen comes up asking if you want to run ridk install, you do.

A "cmd.exe" window appears asking for what you want installed; again the defaults are appropriate.

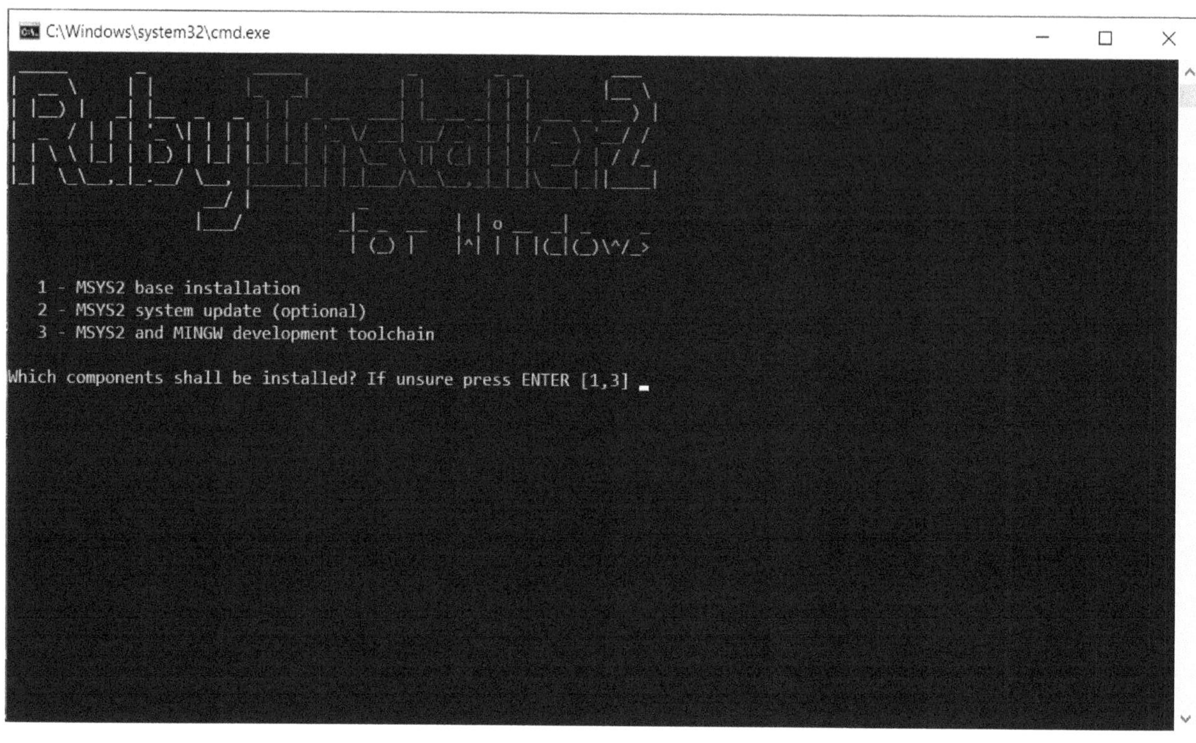

IMG A.4

At the end of that, you will be prompted for what to do next, hitting Enter is appropriate.

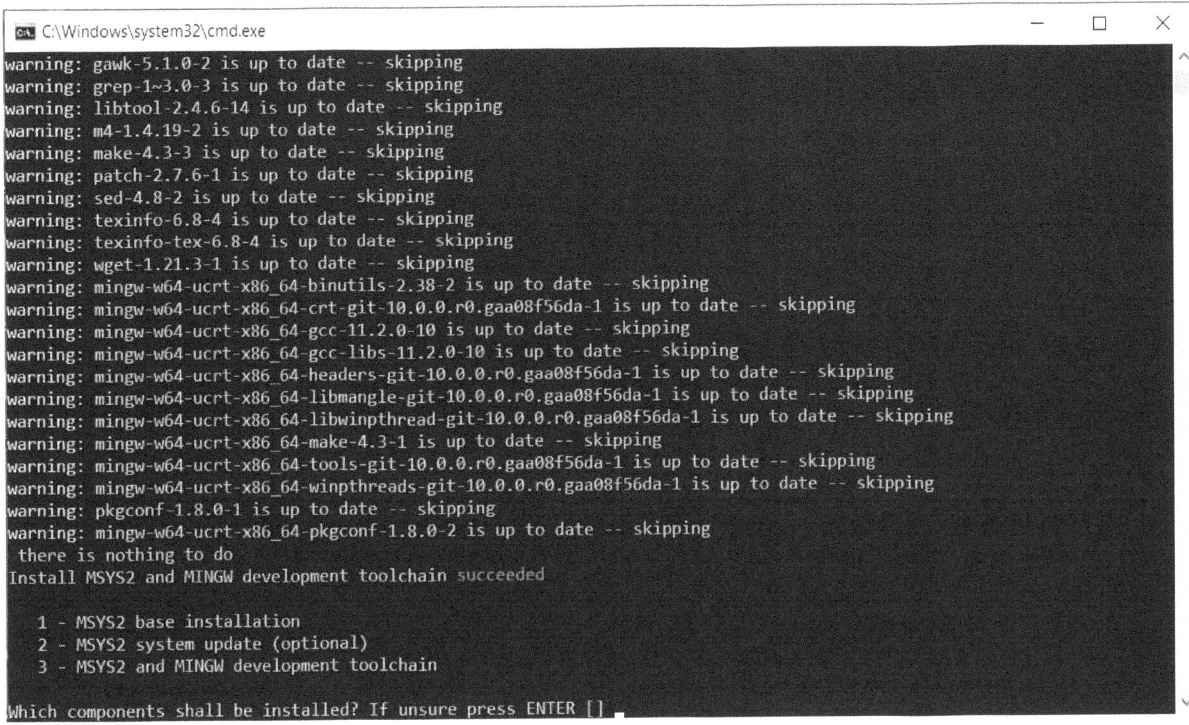

IMG A.5

You can now bring up a PowerShell window and make sure you have a working Ruby.

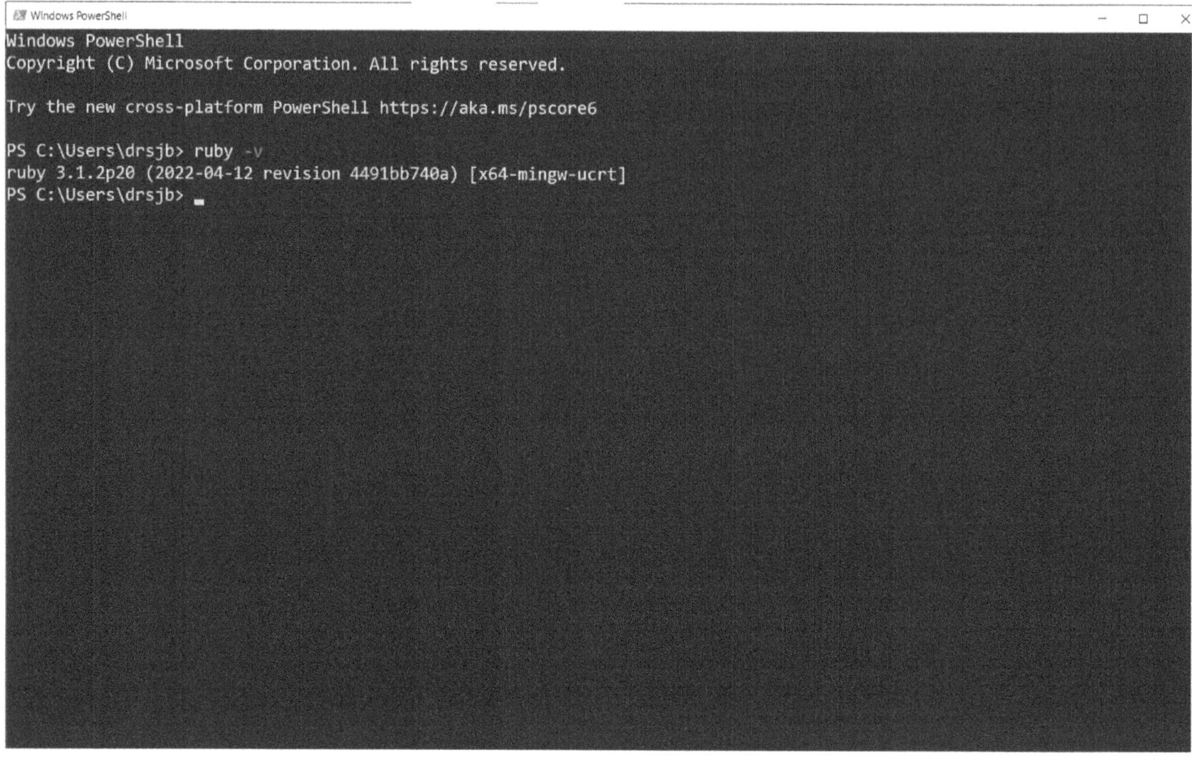

IMG A.6

Generated with PowerShell. Copyright © by Microsoft.

OSX

Macs come with Ruby already installed, but it's not the Ruby you want:

Concept Leads to Code

```
which ruby
/usr/bin/ruby
/usr/bin/ruby --version
ruby 2.6.3p62 (2019-04-16 revision 67580) [universal.x86_64-darwin20]
```

OSX uses Ruby for various system administration tasks, and you don't want to break any of those. Use Homebrew (https://brew.sh/) to install a software manager for the packages you need. It relatively easy to use the instructions on that page. You'll first need to install the XCode command-line utilities: **`xcode-select -install`** and then `/bin/bash -c "$(curl -fsSL` **https://raw.githubusercontent.com/Homebrew/install/HEAD/install.sh**`)"`. You will be prompted for your password so the brew directories can have the correct permissions set. It's recommended that you run `brew doctor` to check that everything is installed correctly. You can then search for the various versions of Ruby Homebrew supports:

Concept Leads to Code

```
brew search ruby
==> Formulae
chruby                              ruby-completion
chruby-fish                         ruby-install
cucumber-ruby                       ruby@2.4
imessage-ruby                       ruby@2.5
jruby                               ruby@2.6
mruby                               ruby@2.7
mruby-cli                           ruby@3.0
rbenv-bundler-ruby-version          rubyfmt
ruby                                 homebrew/portable-ruby/portable-ruby
ruby-build
```

You can then install an appropriate version: **`brew install` ruby@3.0**. Make sure you follow the instructions about adding a path to somewhere in the `/usr/local or /opt` hierarchy to your `.zshrc` or `.bashrc`.

Linux

The directions for Linux are the same as the instructions for the WSL section above.

Install Rails

Now that you have a working version of Ruby, you're set to install Rails. Rails 7 assumes that you have git installed. If you don't, use your OS installer or see https://git-scm.com/downloads. If you don't want to use git, you can pass the `--skip-git` argument to all the `rails new` commands.

Windows and Linux

For these, you should be able to simply do **`gem install rails. A rails –version`** should return something along the lines of `Rails 7.0.3.1`.

And yes, you might have used a software manager (apt) to install a software manager (rbenv) to install a software manager (gem) to install Rails, a bit more complicated than we would hope.

OSX

Make sure you're using the version you install via Homebrew; if you're still pointing to `/usr/bin/ruby`, you won't be able to install rails and will get a permissions error:

Concept Leads to Code

```
ruby --version
ruby 2.6.3p62 (2019-04-16 revision 67580) [universal.x86_64-darwin20]
gem install rails
Fetching crass-1.0.6.gem
Fetching rack-2.2.4.gem
[...]
ERROR:  While executing gem ... (Gem::FilePermissionError)
You don't have write permissions for the /Library/Ruby/Gems/2.6.0 directory.
```

OSX may suggest you do `sudo gem install rails`. **Do not do this!** You can break the system administration tools, something that can be difficult to recover from. Instead, make sure your PATH variable is set to have `/usr/local or /opt/homebrew` before `/usr/bin` and then the installation of Rails should proceed without the need to `sudo`. A **`which ruby`** should return `/usr/local/opt/ruby/bin/ruby` or `~/.rbenv/shims/ruby` or similar depending on how you installed Ruby. Once Rails is installed, you might have to add the path to the directory where the various Rails executables are, e.g.: **`echo 'export PATH="/usr/local/lib/ruby/gems/3.1.0/bin:$PATH"' >> ~/.zshrc`**. However, the actual path will vary depending on the version you install and the shell you are using.

Test Your Installation

You can now create a very simple application via the following.

Concept Leads to Code

```
rails new demo
cd demo
rails server
```

Here's what it should look like in PowerShell, though it will look similar on all platforms.

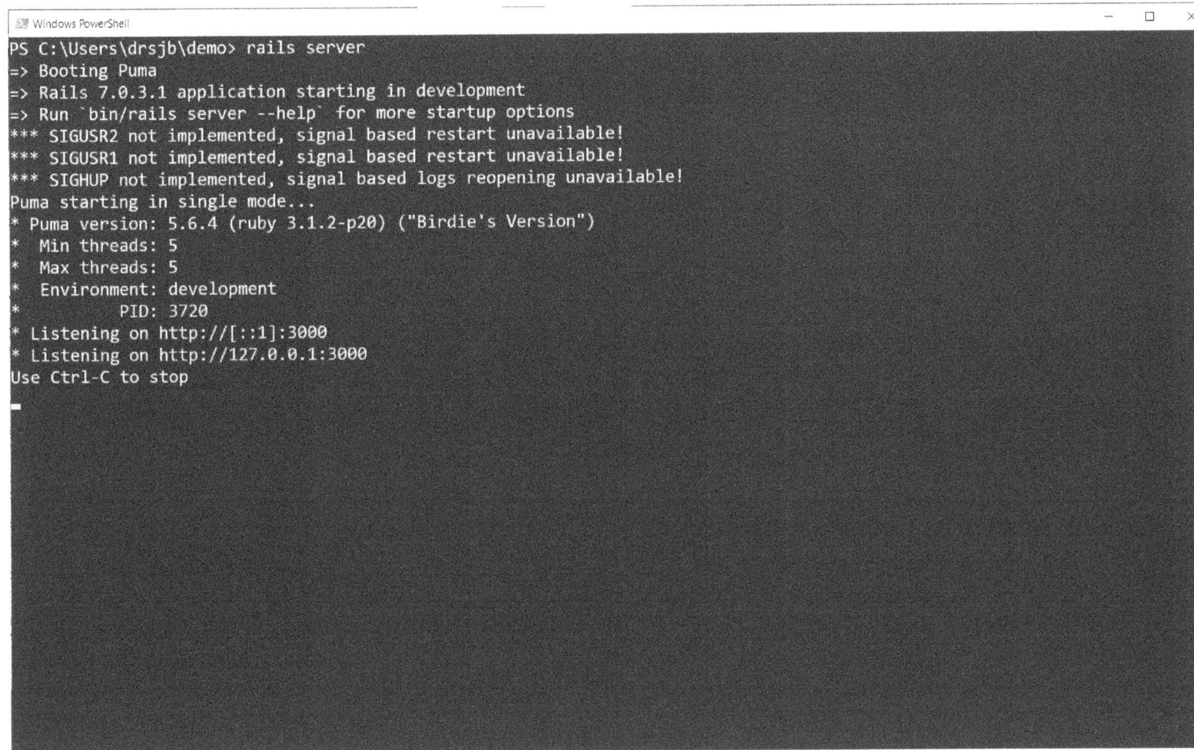

IMG A.7

Generated with PowerShell. Copyright © by Microsoft.

Point your browser at http://127.0.0.1:3000 and that should show the following.

Rails version: 7.0.3.1
Ruby version: ruby 3.1.2p20 (2022-04-12 revision 4491bb740a) [x64-mingw-ucrt]

IMG A.8

Once you're doing experimenting, type Control-C in the terminal to stop the server; here's what that should look like.

```
Windows PowerShell

Started GET "/" for ::1 at 2022-07-14 10:00:01 -0600
Processing by Rails::WelcomeController#index as HTML
  Rendering C:/Ruby31-x64/lib/ruby/gems/3.1.0/gems/railties-7.0.3.1/lib/rails/templates/rails/welcome/index.html.erb
  Rendered C:/Ruby31-x64/lib/ruby/gems/3.1.0/gems/railties-7.0.3.1/lib/rails/templates/rails/welcome/index.html.erb (Dur
ation: 1.0ms | Allocations: 307)
Completed 200 OK in 4ms (Views: 2.0ms | ActiveRecord: 0.0ms | Allocations: 997)


Started GET "/" for ::1 at 2022-07-14 10:00:08 -0600
Processing by Rails::WelcomeController#index as HTML
  Rendering C:/Ruby31-x64/lib/ruby/gems/3.1.0/gems/railties-7.0.3.1/lib/rails/templates/rails/welcome/index.html.erb
  Rendered C:/Ruby31-x64/lib/ruby/gems/3.1.0/gems/railties-7.0.3.1/lib/rails/templates/rails/welcome/index.html.erb (Dur
ation: 0.2ms | Allocations: 29)
Completed 200 OK in 7ms (Views: 4.1ms | ActiveRecord: 0.0ms | Allocations: 280)


Started GET "/" for ::1 at 2022-07-14 10:01:11 -0600
Processing by Rails::WelcomeController#index as HTML
  Rendering C:/Ruby31-x64/lib/ruby/gems/3.1.0/gems/railties-7.0.3.1/lib/rails/templates/rails/welcome/index.html.erb
  Rendered C:/Ruby31-x64/lib/ruby/gems/3.1.0/gems/railties-7.0.3.1/lib/rails/templates/rails/welcome/index.html.erb (Dur
ation: 0.5ms | Allocations: 29)
Completed 200 OK in 8ms (Views: 6.4ms | ActiveRecord: 0.0ms | Allocations: 252)


- Gracefully stopping, waiting for requests to finish
=== puma shutdown: 2022-07-14 10:30:31 -0600 ===
- Goodbye!
Exiting
Terminate batch job (Y/N)? y
PS C:\Users\drsjb\demo>
```

IMG A.9

Generated with PowerShell. Copyright © by Microsoft.

Cross-Platform

Web-Based

Some sites allow you to develop RoR applications via a web browser that are either free or for very little cost. Here are several, though it must be noted that these types of sites come and go through the years and there are many others worth considering.

- https://replit.com/
- https://codeanywhere.com/

Docker

Docker (https://www.docker.com/) is a widely used container-based approach to **development** and deployment. It allows the creation of lightweight "virtual machines" (really: *containers*) that can run easily on many different platforms. If you already have it installed or are interested in exploring its capabilities, this approach is for you. As the Windows version of Docker requires WSL (above), this method requires a version of Windows above the Home Version; e.g.: Education or Pro. For Linux and OSX, there are free community editions of Docker available for installation. There is a simple Docker image for developing RoR applications in the central Docker repository; here is the Docker file that generates a **development environment**.

Concept Leads to Code

```
FROM alpine 3.18
MAINTAINER Dr. Steve Beaty
EXPOSE 3000
VOLUME ["/home"]
RUN apk update
RUN apk upgrade
RUN apk add --upgrade ruby ruby-dev
RUN apk add build-base zlib-dev git
RUN apk add sqlite sqlite-dev tzdata
RUN apk add yaml-dev
RUN gem install rails
WORKDIR /home
```

To run, do`docker run --platform linux/x86_64 -it -p 3000:3000 -v ${PWD}:/home drsjb80/rails-dev`. You'll have to run the Rails commands in the container and specifically in the `/home` directory, but you can point your editor/IDE at the created directory on the host machine. It's easiest to run the Rails server bound to all IP addresses via `rails server -b 0.0.0.0`. Here's an example running in a container.

Concept Leads to Code

```
rails new demo
      create
      create  README.md
      create  Rakefile
      create  .ruby-version
[...]
Appending: pin "@hotwired/stimulus-loading", to: "stimulus-loading.js", preload: 
true
      append  config/importmap.rb
Pin all controllers
Appending: pin_all_from "app/javascript/controllers", under: "controllers"
      append  config/importmap.rb
cd demo
rails server -b 0.0.0.0
=> Booting Puma
=> Rails 7.0.3.1 application starting in development
=> Run `bin/rails server --help` for more startup options
Puma starting in single mode...
* Puma version: 5.6.4 (ruby 3.1.2-p20) ("Birdie's Version")
*  Min threads: 5
*  Max threads: 5
*  Environment: development
*          PID: 403
* Listening on http://0.0.0.0:3000
Use Ctrl-C to stop
```

There will now be a `demo` folder in the host machine where you ran the `docker run` command with the Rails application that you can modify. You can point your browser at http://127.0.0.1:3000 to see the running Rails server.

Starting with Rails 7.1, a Dockerfile is automatically created that you can modify and use. Here is an improved version of the file that works in development mode.

Concept Leads to Code

```
# syntax = docker/dockerfile:1

ARG RUBY_VERSION=3.2.2
FROM registry.docker.com/library/ruby:$RUBY_VERSION-slim as base

# The Rails app lives here in Docker.
WORKDIR /rails

# Don't set the production environment as you'll need (at least) an SSL
# self-signed cert and this Dockerfile doesn't do that.

FROM base as build

RUN apt-get update -qq && \
    apt-get install --no-install-recommends -y build-essential git libvips pkg-
config

COPY Gemfile Gemfile.lock ./
RUN bundle install && \
    rm -rf ~/.bundle/ "${BUNDLE_PATH}"/ruby/*/cache
"${BUNDLE_PATH}"/ruby/*/bundler/gems/*/.git && \
    bundle exec bootsnap precompile --gemfile

# Copy the files already here to the image. It might really be better to
# use a volume.
COPY . .

RUN bundle exec bootsnap precompile app/ lib/

RUN SECRET_KEY_BASE_DUMMY=1 ./bin/rails assets:precompile

FROM base

RUN apt-get update -qq && \
  apt-get install --no-install-recommends -y curl libsqlite3-0 libvips && \
  rm -rf /var/lib/apt/lists /var/cache/apt/archives

COPY --from=build /usr/local/bundle /usr/local/bundle
COPY --from=build /rails /rails

# Run and own only the runtime files as a non-root user for security and
# add the /rails directory.
RUN useradd rails --create-home --shell /bin/bash && \
    chown -R rails:rails db log storage tmp /rails
USER rails:rails

ENTRYPOINT ["/rails/bin/docker-entrypoint"]

# Start the server by default, and add binding to a port so it works on
# OSX.
EXPOSE 3000
CMD ["./bin/rails", "server", "-b", "0.0.0.0"]
```

Here are the commands you can use to leverage the Dockerfile.

Concept Leads to Code

```
rails new docker
cd docker
docker build -t railsdocker .
docker run -it -p 3000:3000 --env RAILS_MASTER_KEY=`cat config/master.key`
railsdocker
```

Rails Server Environments

The Rails server has three modes of operation: development, **testing**, and production. Each can be specified when the server starts using either the `-e` or `--environment=` arguments. We'll be using the development mode in this book for everything but testing, and development is the default. Test mode is used for running the tests we write and run using the server. Test mode, among other actions, creates its own database with predictable values for testing. Production mode emphasizes speed over the flexibility we want while developing. It disallows certain messages to the user that may help developers but expose too much information to malicious actors, e.g.: full error messages are not shown to users in production mode. Full caching is enabled, meaning that changes to the source code will not immediately be reflected in the application. Compression of CSS and JavaScript is enabled in production mode, making the reading and debugging of both somewhat more complicated. The specific configurations for each of the environments can be found in the `config/environments` directory, in files named `development.rb`, `production.rb`, and `test.rb`.

Summary

We've found several ways to create a development environment for Ruby on Rails. While creating stable and useful development, testing, and production environments is rarely trivial, they are crucial to building web applications. It is also important that whatever environment you choose, your team's collaboration tools and repositories are easily accessible in that environment. RoR has plugins and tools available for most Integrated Development Environments (IDEs) so choose your favorite or experiment to find one that works best for you.

Exercises

Directions: Use what you learned in this chapter to complete the following tasks and exercises.

1. Get a working RoR development environment by installing one on your local machine.
2. Use a Docker container to create a RoR development environment.
3. Experiment with a web-based RoR environment to learn the benefits and detriments of such an environment.

Index

1-to-1. *See* one-to-one
1-to-many. *See* one-to-many
2FA, 121

A

abstraction, 14, 15, 18, 27, 96
accept, 7, 8, 10, 78
accessible, 2, 29, 67, 68
Ajax. *See* Asynchronous JavaScript And XML
API. *See* Application Programming Interfaces
Application Programming Interfaces (API), 81
Asynchronous JavaScript And XML (AJAX), 82
authentication, 5, 9–10, 121
auth/n, 121
authorization, 121, 122, 123
auth/z, 121

B

Bad Request, 9
BDD. *See* Behavior Driven Development
Behavior Driven Development (BDD), 84
browser security, 124

C

CA. *See* certificate authorities
Cascading Style Sheets (CSS), 3, 4, 37, 67, 69, 70, 73, 75, 76, 82, 90, 91, 96, 125, 151
certificate authorities (CA), 124
channels, 53, 101
chasing references, 62
CI/CD. *See* Continuous Integration/Continuous Deployment
client/server, 2, 37, 113
close, 2, 8
Continuous Integration/Continuous Deployment (CI/CD), 52, 76, 128
convention over configuration, 37
cookies, 1, 5, 10, 113, 114

CORS. *See* Cross-Origin Resource Sharing
Cross-Origin Resource Sharing (CORS), 125, 126
Cross-Site Request Forgery (CSRF), 87, 128
cross-site scripting (XSS), 119, 128–129
CSRF. *See* Cross-Site Request Forgery
CSS. *See* Cascading Style Sheets

D

dark web, 130, 131
deep web, 130, 131
dependency injection, 36, 55
Document Object Model (DOM), 3, 90, 91, 92
DOM. *See* Document Object Model
Domain-Specific Languages (DSL), 82–83
Don't Repeat Yourself (DRY), 70, 74, 103, 114
DRY. *See* Don't Repeat Yourself
DSL. *See* Domain-Specific Languages
duck typing, 90

E

embedding, 62, 63
encapsulation, 18–19
eXtensible Markup Language (XML), 3, 37, 82, 94

F

factors, 121, 122
File Transfer Protocol (FTP), 2, 10, 113
first normal form, 59
Forbidden, 10
FTP. *See* File Transfer Protocol
full-stack, 94

G

generators, 32, 39
Gopher, 2
Go To Statement Considered Harmful, 18

H

HABTM. *See* has_and_belongs_to_many
has_and_belongs_to_many (HABTM), 50, 51, 54, 70
hash, 17–18, 79, 107, 114
has_many_through, 50
highly coherent, 19
hooks, 94
HTML. *See* Hyper Text Markup Language
HTTP. *See* Hypertext Transfer Protocol
HTTP over the wire, 80, 82

HTTPS, 10, 114, 123–124
Hypertext, 1, 2, 5
Hyper Text Markup Language (HTML), 2, 3–4, 7, 8, 10, 11, 36, 67, 68–70, 73, 75, 76, 78, 79, 81, 82, 90–91, 94, 96, 103, 106, 107, 108, 122, 128
Hypertext Transfer Protocol (HTTP), 2, 5–11, 12, 69, 106, 108, 113, 123, 125
Hypertext Transfer Protocol – HTTP/1.1, 5, 7, 8, 9

I

inheritance, 14, 21, 90
injection, 36–37, 55–56, 94, 107, 108, 126, 127, 128
Internal Server Error, 10
Internationalization, 71
internet, 2, 5, 7, 119, 130
inter-process communication (IPC), 101
IPC. *See* inter-process communication

J

JavaScript Object Notation (JSON), 7, 9, 11, 36, 59–60, 69, 80, 81–103
JavaScript XML (JSX), 94
JIT. *See* Just in Time
JSON. *See* JavaScript Object Notation
JSX. *See* JavaScript XML
Just in Time (JIT), 76

K

keep-alive, 8

L

localization, 71
look and feel, 75
loosely coupled, 19

M

mass assignment, 107–108
metaprogramming, 67, 74
Method Not Allowed, 10
MFA. *See* Multifactor Authentication
migrations, 31, 32, 33, 35, 39
mixins, 21, 22
Multifactor Authentication (MFA), 121
multiple inheritance, 21
mustaches, 91

N

Node Package Manager (npm), 98
non-relational databases, 30, 36, 59, 64
normalization, 59
Not Acceptable, 10
Not Found, 9–10
Not Implemented, 10
Not Modified, 6, 9
npm. *See* Node Package Manager

O

Object-Oriented Programming languages (OOP), 13, 14–26
on-demand, 76
one-to-many, 39, 51–52, 60, 62
one-to-one, 39, 46, 51–52, 60
OOP. *See* Object-Oriented Programming languages

P

Personally Identifiable Information (PII), 128, 132
PII. *See* Personally Identifiable Information
polymorphism, 24
Progressive Web Application (PWA), 90–91
PWA. *See* Progressive Web Application

R

responsive, 75

S

Same-Origin Policy (SOP), 124–125, 128
SectionsStudents, 50, 51
See Other, 9
self-signed certificate, 123
separation of concerns, 36, 75, 91, 94
sigils, 19
Simple Object Access Protocol (SOAP), 82
single inheritance, 21
SOAP. *See* Simple Object Access Protocol
SOP. *See* Same-Origin Policy
SQLi. *See* SQL injections
SQL injections (SQLi), 126–127
surface web, 130, 131, 132

T

TCP/IP, 2, 5, 8
TDD. *See* Test-Driven Development

Test-Driven Development (TDD), 52–53
two-way binding, 91, 92

U

UI/UX. *See* user interface/user experience
Unauthorized, 9
user interface/user experience (UI/UX), 67

W

WAIS. *See* Wide Area Information Server
weakly typed, 90
web application framework, 36–37
web sockets, 80
Wide Area Information Server (WAIS), 2

XML. *See* eXtensible Markup Language
XSS. *See* cross-site scripting

Ya Ain't Gonna Need It (YAGNI), 52
YAGNI. *See* Ya Ain't Gonna Need It
YAML, 53, 71, 85, 115, 121
YAML Ain't Markup Language. *See* YAML
Yet Another Markup Language. *See* YAML

www.ingramcontent.com/pod-product-compliance
Ingram Content Group UK Ltd.
Pitfield, Milton Keynes, MK11 3LW, UK
UKHW061702190726
13853UKWH00008B/2358